I0117777

BRAND*cebo*

BRAND*cebo*

The Powerful Placebo Effect of Brands

And its impact on our behavior

and performance

Doron Malka

mamalima

PUBLISHING

Mamalima Publishing
11665 Avena Place #205
San Diego, CA 92128
www.mamalima.com

Ordering Information:
Quantity sales. Special discounts are available on quantity purchases by corporations, associations, and others.
For details, contact the publisher at the address above.

Printed in the United States of America

LIBRARY OF CONGRESS CATALOGING-IN-PUBLICATION DATA
Doron Malka
BRAND*cebo*: the powerful placebo effect of brands and its impact on our behavior and performance / Doron Malka p. cm.

LIBRARY OF CONGRESS CONTROL NUMBER: 2017949410

ISBN 978-0-9992274-0-4

1. Branding—Psychological aspects. 2. Marketing—Psychological aspects.
3. Consumer Behavior —Psychological aspects. I. Title.

First Edition

Cover design by Sarah Schmidt, Ameba Marketing, Inc.

10 9 8 7 6 5 4 3 2 1

To the mega brands that started it all,
my parents,
Rosette and Albert Malka

And to my constant source
of purpose and passion,
my wife, Ursula, and my kids,
Matan, Maya, Sophia and Lior

TABLE OF CONTENTS

INTRODUCTION

Let me tell you a story. It begins in 1973. I was a seven-year-old boy in Jerusalem, and my parents bought me a new pair of Adidas®, the most talked-about brand of running shoes in my school.

"These shoes are so fast!" I boasted to my friends as I darted up and down our street, confident that I'd become a faster runner.

Fourteen-year-old Calvin Cambridge experienced much the same phenomenon in the movie *Like Mike*[1]. The New York-City orphan was passionate about basketball and idolized Michael Jordan. His ultimate dream was to play in the NBA, but he was too short and his limited ball-handling skills hardly made him a challenger to his neighborhood playmates. That is, until one day he laced up a pair of old basketball sneakers with the initials "MJ" stamped inside them.

Calvin was convinced that the sneakers once belonged to the legendary Michael Jordan. His belief transformed him into a basketball superstar as he discovered in himself new skills that made his dream of becoming an NBA star come true.

Obviously, I'm not suggesting that you run out and buy a pair of Air Jordans to make your basketball fantasies come true. I am, however, saying that Calvin's fictional "BRAND*cebo*" experience is not as far-fetched as we might believe.

"BRAND*cebo*" is my term for the placebo effect of brands. While we may be familiar with the use of the term "placebo" in the context of drug trials, the term's use in marketing is brand new.

Scientists long ago discovered that a patient's expectations for the effect of the drug, which may be nothing more than an inert capsule, has the power to affect the "drug's" ability to deliver the desired effect. That's why drugs that are tested must outperform the base placebo effect to demonstrate their effectiveness. What we now know is that successful brands have power over consumers akin to the effect of placebos.

As a part of my doctoral dissertation, I conducted an experiment into the placebo effect of brands. The methodology of that experiment and its profound outcomes are detailed in Chapter 1. The bottom line (spoiler alert!) is that I was able to prove that youngsters run faster when they wear Nike shoes. Not just a little faster—significantly faster.

But the placebo effect of brands doesn't only work on impressionable adolescents. A 2015 study by three business school professors examined the ability of performance brands (brands that enable activities that have measurable outcomes) to cause a placebo effect[2].

The professors invited amateur golfers to test a new golf putter. Half of the participants were told they would be putting with a Nike putter, while the other half were not told which brand of putter they would be using. In reality, all participants in the experiment used the exact same putter, yet the golfers who thought they were playing with a Nike putter suddenly experienced improved skills and needed significantly fewer putts to win the hole.

The Nike brand had had its placebo effect, significantly improving adults' putting scores, just as Calvin's belief that he was wearing Michael Jordan's discarded basketball sneakers made him a better basketball player. The way his belief influenced his performance doesn't sound so crazy now.

In this book, I provide additional, equally compelling examples of the brand placebo phenomenon. From research demonstrating how consumers' pre-established fondness for a particular beer disappears when they consume the same beer under a different label[3] to individuals rating the taste of Coke dramatically lower when they consume it from an unbranded cup[4], conclusive empirical findings have led to the acceptance of the placebo effect. The placebo effect of brands is no longer viewed as a self-fulfilling prophecy but as a valuable driver of consumer behavior.

BRAND*cebo* coalesces and solidifies five decades of research into the placebo effect of brands. It also identifies each of the three critical ingredients that enable a brand to have a brand placebo effect while introducing breakthrough brand placebo implications that were not previously studied.

Working on this book led me to dig deep into my own over 20 years of brand-building experience at my agency, Ameba Marketing. To my surprise, I discovered that I had been subconsciously but effectively using elements of the brand placebo effect even in our early branding work. As I became more immersed in experiments with brand priming (a specific element of the brand placebo effect) and other techniques, I began using these elements more consciously in almost every branding campaign we created.

At its core, BRAND*cebo* represents a challenge to traditional marketing concepts that attribute changes in consumer behavior to strategic changes associated with product, price, promotion, and place (the four Ps of marketing) that have been the centerpieces of marketing practice for many decades. Traditional marketing strategies focus primarily on manipulating one or more of the four Ps independent of their targeted audience's cognitive and emotional experiences.

BRAND*cebo* unequivocally demonstrates that this traditional axiom of consumerism is largely obsolete. Instead, it suggests that consumers' buying behavior could be greatly affected by branding strategies that focus on psychological, cognitive, and emotional attributes.

BRAND*cebo* offers a dramatic shift in the way we think about brands and the intimate relationships we have with them. As such, I hope it inspires further research and healthy debate.

ENJOY.

Chapter 1

The Road to BRAND*cebo*:
A Childhood Experience Turned Branding Phenomenon

My childhood experience with the running shoes was the first time I experienced the placebo effects of brands, but over the years, I've realized that I was not alone in believing that certain brands imbued their users with almost "magical" powers. My personal experience left an impression that has been part of my consciousness throughout my professional life.

Okay, I admit it: I'm a sucker for brands. They had power over me then, and they have power over me now. Subconsciously (perhaps...), in almost every purchasing decision I make, the rational part of my brain concedes to the emotional part.

As a marketing professional, I not only recognize this conflict, but also have studied it enough so that I'm convinced it's true. I am fascinated by the obscure ability of something abstract to elicit in me emotions so profound and real that they dictate my actions. Like visual arts, poetry, or music, the philosophical and emotional meanings of brands are created in the minds of the viewer, the reader, and the listener, and take hold of their hearts. Their interpretations are different and unique, thereby ensuring the longevity and eternal fascination with what they represent.

I knew how people reacted to brands and how powerfully a brand name affected me. Was it possible that what I had experienced as a seven-year old with his first pair of Adidas running shoes was a "brand placebo" effect—a BRAND*cebo*?

Whether we're conscious of it or not, brands work their way into our culture, psyches, and even language. For example, Shakespeare lived almost 450 years ago, yet to this day, his brand name conveys an impression of writing excellence.

Brands can also function as metaphors. When we describe a sunflower as a "van Gogh sunflower," we communicate that that flower has an essence of "sunflowerness" even if it is not the largest or most attractive sunflower we've ever seen.

Similarly, imagine someone says to you, "Wow, you look like a million bucks!"

Admit it. You actually feel it. You walk a bit taller, your step is a bit surer, your chest a bit fuller, and your voice louder and more confident. You probably feel pretty good about yourself—proud for choosing that outfit or the brand of clothing you're wearing.

Research now shows that those feelings aren't only in your head. The moment that you went to your closet to choose that outfit or that brand of jacket, dress, or slacks, you gained more confidence in yourself. On a physiological level, your shoulders physically pulled back and your chest opened up. Brands cast a powerful spell that helps us project who we are or who we want to become.

We all know people (none of them your friends, of course) who, when complimented on their outfit, shoes, or jewelry impulsively share the brand name.

"I love that dress you're wearing," you might say.

"Thank you. It's Armani," they respond. If they haven't volunteered it, you might even ask for the brand name because you're dying to know what makes the wearer look so good. When we love a brand, we feel better and more confident when wearing or using it.

Unlike other forms of art in which the audience bestows its admiration upon its creator—the painter, poet, or composer—successful brands elicit self-actualized feelings within us. At its most successful, a brand we use reflects the best expression of who we are, or how we would like to be perceived.

After nearly a quarter century of being intimately involved in all levels of brand development and communication, I look at commercials, print advertisements, product packaging, and other brand expressions, and know immediately what they want me to feel and believe. I understand the direct and subliminal cognitive manipulation at work (they're not all bad), and yet I still fall for them. I'm fascinated by their ability to create new realities that invite the viewer or consumer to dwell happily upon a brand for 15, 30, or even 60 seconds. I admire brands' ability to develop intimate relationships with consumers who occasionally attribute traits to the brands they love because of how they want to see themselves.

THE BIRTH OF AN IDEA

I'm fascinated by how we think and make decisions, and how marketing can affect both. Throughout my career I have been convinced that "marketing" is much more a study of human behavior than it is a business practice.

At the same time, I've been fascinated for years by the placebo effect in medicine. I was amazed that people could experience a physiological change in response to their expectations and beliefs. Placebos trigger real, physiological, chemical reactions in our body to combat our headache, depression, and other medical ailments. And what's more, half of all drugs that fail in late-stage trials drop out of the pipeline due to their inability to exceed the effects of sugar pills[5].

This took me back to my childhood experience with my branded running shoes. Did I really run faster or was it all in my head? It got me wondering whether the same phenomenon—the placebo affect—might apply to brands.

I needed to know, but I quickly realized that despite the prevalence of brands in our daily lives, relatively little scientific investigation has been conducted in the area of placebo effects and marketing. Despite the placebo effect's undisputed recognition in the medical field, as evidenced by its mandated use by the Food and Drug Administration (FDA) as a control method in every clinical study for a new drug (to earn FDA approval, a new medication must beat the placebo's results in at least two placebo-controlled, double-blinded Phase 3 trials), it is viewed with skepticism in other fields.

The little research I did find was fascinating. It appears that consumers' fondness for a particular beer disappears when they consume the same beer under a different label[6]. Similarly, individuals rate the taste of Coke dramatically lower when the cola was consumed from an unbranded cup[7]. And women experience an increased body temperature when wearing a Hermes-labeled shawl versus wearing the same shawl without a label.

This made it clear that the placebo effect wasn't an ignored expression of a self-fulfilling prophecy, but an *important driver of consumer behavior.* This is what warrants the investment companies make in their brands, why each brand needs to adhere to a consistent message, and why companies so zealously protect their brands.

Furthermore, within the limited research that has been conducted on the placebo effect and brands, I found that no effective practical application of this phenomenon was offered to me, as a marketer. So I decided to pursue it myself.

My doctoral studies gave me an opportunity to answer my many questions. Even before taking my first class, I knew the topic of my dissertation: *The Placebo Effect of Brands.*

The word "placebo" comes from the Latin phrase "I shall please.[8]" When patients' belief that they were receiving a powerful drug began to show its effect in the results of clinical trials, drug companies started using inert substances, such as sugar or starch[9], in a capsule that resembled the actual capsule being tested. Recently, drug companies have been using substances that cause the same side effects as the drug being tested, or another drug to which they are comparing a new medication.

Studying the phenomenon as it occurred in drug trials, I discovered that three critical elements contribute to the placebo effect.

The first element is *Conditioning* (or, *Priming,* as I refer to it in marketing terms): the patient's strong belief in the medical effectiveness of the drug the doctor prescribes.

The second element is *Expectation:* the patient's own conviction that the drug will yield the desired effect.

The final element involves motivation*:* the patient's natural *Desire* to feel better. That gives the patient in the trial a vested interest in experiencing the drug's effectiveness.

Each of these elements is subconscious. In drug trials, neither the doctor nor the patient knows whether he or she is receiving the actual drug being tested or an inert substance that resembles it. Placebos are carefully designed to look exactly like the real thing, so that there is no ability to detect which drug contains the active ingredient and which contains an inert substance that would have no effect on the body.

To illustrate this placebo effect, imagine going to the doctor with a pounding headache. The doctor recommends a "magical pill" that has been effective with 99% of his patients who suffered from migraine headaches. You trust your doctor, believing (*Priming)* that the pill works magic on powerful headaches. Now, since the doctor said it worked for 99% of his patients, you fully *expect (Expectation)* that it will work for you, as well. And let's face it: you're absolutely dying to get rid of this headache (*Desire).* That "magical pill" could contain a substance that would have no medical effect on the body, but the headache is gone! That, my friend, is the placebo effect.

Could brands also have this effect on consumers, just as I had experienced? Could strong brand recognition create consumer *Priming* ("I love this brand of running shoes") that, coupled with *Expectation* ("I bet I can run faster with these shoes") and *Desire* ("I really want to run faster"), would directly affect the performance of the product. I wanted to learn how this phenomenon worked in marketing and how I could replicate it for my own clients.

Finally, I wanted to understand the longevity characteristics of the placebo effect of brands. Were the physiological effects permanent or limited to the time of exposure? Would they carry over as long as the consumer is under the same Priming, Expectation, and Desire? But on that, later.

PUTTING CHILD'S PLAY TO THE (ACADEMIC) TEST

Did my journey into brand exploration start with that pair of running shoes? I have no idea, but 40 years later, in my pursuit for deeper understanding of the science of marketing, I continued to explore that same phenomenon, that deep belief that my Adidas shoes made me a better runner. And my doctoral studies were the perfect grounds for that exploration. I believe I was the only doctoral candidate who had the topic of his dissertation down even before program orientation.

I decided to investigate the BRAND*cebo* effect on youths aged nine to thirteen, or the "tween" cohort as they are referred to by marketers. Why this demographic segment? First, because I owed the younger version of myself an answer to the question that started it all: did that highly desired brand of running shoes *really* make me run faster? Second, during the ages of nine to thirteen-years old, most youngsters are brand conscious, and use brands to establish social status and acceptance.

They are also the current and future makers and breakers of brands. This demographic cohort consists of over 20 million boys and girls in the U.S. alone, and is directly and indirectly responsible for about $200 billion of spending per year[10]. If brands truly possess placebo power, they will surely work their magic on this age group.

Previous studies of the placebo effect in marketing have focused on impacts of changing or manipulating one element of the marketing mix, typically price, as consumers are likely to perceive a higher-priced product as being of higher quality. The main drivers studied have been the three elements I described earlier (and that I cover in more detail in later chapters): Priming, Expectation, and Desire. When combined, these three factors have enormous power over the human mind and body. They exert the powerful effect of the placebo, or in the case of this book, the BRAND*cebo* effect.

While my study was built upon some of those principles, it particularly focused on brand recognition and perception as triggers of a placebo effect, as was shown earlier with consumers' reactions to unbranded beer, Coke, and an Hermes shawl.

Specifically, my study focused on the extent to which children's recognition of a particular brand of running shoes and their positive perceptions of that brand affected their performance in a 50-meter run.

My first hypothesis was that participants who are exposed (through promotional materials) to the superior attributes of the brand and then use that brand would experience a placebo effect that would positively affect their performance in the 50-meter run. Simply put, they would run faster.

The second hypothesis was that those children who are also exposed to the superior attributes of the brand but did *not* use it in the experiment would have their performance in the 50-meter run negatively affected. They would run more slowly. The indirect impact of a desired brand over the performance of competing brands is what I call the *Ricochet Effect.* (I describe it in detail in Chapter 7.)

I further hypothesized that following education on the superior attributes of the brand (Priming), there would be a significant difference in Expectation and Desire levels between participants who were allowed to use the brand and those who were not allowed to use it. The objective of my study was to show that both Expectation and Desire would directly affect performance. These are two fundamental components of the strongest placebos.

Finally, I wanted to see if time since the exposure might be an important factor in sustaining the positive results of the Placebo Effect and the negative results due to the Ricochet Effect. My gut told me that the effects generated by positive perception of the brand would diminish over time.

I divided my study into two phases to test my hypotheses. The first experiment would demonstrate whether the Placebo and Ricochet Effects were created by brand recognition and perception, and what role Expectation and Motivation played in that process.

The second experiment was conducted seven days later and specifically investigated whether performance levels affected by Placebo and Ricochet Effects in the first study held up over time.

DOES THE NIKE BRAND HAVE A PLACEBO EFFECT?

I approached two schools in San Diego and recruited 100 boys and 100 girls between the ages of nine and thirteen —an age of transition between childhood and adolescence—to participate in an experiment.

Tweens' straightforward, well-informed, and well-defined sense of style is critical to the success of brands that target them and the emergence of effective future brands. This might explain why marketers spend an estimated $17 billion annually to grab their attention and loyalty. Could the power of the BRAND*cebo* make a real and measurable difference in their running performance?

I first needed to establish a baseline by measuring how fast the recruited youths could run without any intervention. So with the help of their PE teachers, we defined a 50-meter course on the school's running track. Wearing the shoes they ordinarily wore for running, the youngsters ran the 50-meter course in groups of two or four. Their times were recorded.

Fifteen minutes later, they reran the same course wearing a pair of Nike Free Run 5.0 shoes, but for this test, I had disguised the brand marking so that the shoes looked like unbranded, cheap knockoffs.

I chose Nike because it has the strongest brand awareness, recognition, and stature of any other running shoe on the planet. During the 2016 fiscal year, Nike spent over $850 million on "demand creation[11]." The students' running time with the "knockoff" shoes was also recorded.

First step accomplished; I had my baseline measures of their running speeds both in their own shoes and in my brand-disguised Nikes. Now it was time to test the power of BRAND*cebo*.

Nike Free Run 5.0[12]

I dramatically displayed a brand-new pair of Nike Free Run 5.0 shoes and asked all the runners to read to themselves a brief passage that clearly identified the shoes I'd brought for them to wear as Nike products and described the features of these shoes. It spoke glowingly of the "foot strengthening benefits of natural motion, along with the cushioning, traction, and underfoot protection" the shoe would provide. It spoke of the "smooth, efficient stride" runners would attain. I further told them that people who run with these Nike shoes improve their running speed, on average, by 20%.

It was essentially a Nike advertisement, a microscopic dose of the promotional information youngsters consume each day as they watch television, play computer games, listen to music, read magazines, go to sports events, and explore the world online. In fact, it is estimated that children between the ages of two and eleven see an average of 25,600 ads a year[13]. What impact would this one tiny twitch of the Nike brand's magic wand have on these ad-swamped kids' ability to run? To find out, I would need to time them on the same course again.

To accomplish this, I randomly divided the kids into two groups. One group would run wearing the Nikes that had undergone a surgical "brandectomy" that left them looking like any other cheap knockoff but still had every physical feature of the shoe intact. The other group would proudly don Nikes bearing the famed "swoosh" logo and the full power of the brand's advertising messages.

Before their next run, though—but after each group had read the Nike promotional material—I asked both groups to complete two short questionnaires. One asked how much they *expected* the Nike-branded shoe to improve their running times while the other asked how much they *wanted* the Nike-branded shoe to improve their running times. (Later in this book, we will explore why Expectation and Desire are such critical factors in the BRAND*cebo* effect.)

I could have stopped there; after all, what I was interested in were their running times and seeing if being exposed to the promotional material made any difference in them. But I took the experiment one step further.

To see if any measurable effect lasted over time, I returned to the same schools one week later and re-tested the students, timing them on the same course while wearing their own shoes, just as I had at the beginning of the study.

Then I sat with my computer for some pretty serious statistical number crunching: Cronbach alpha statistic tests, coefficient intervals, t-tests, Mann-Whitney-Wilcoxon tests... Don't ask. You don't want to know. (See Appendix A if you do.)

But what you *do* want to know, and what this book is really about, is what is already affecting you every day, not only in your business but also in your life.

What I found out is that the BRAND*cebo* effect was real enough to reach into those kids' bodies and pump up their muscles' ability to propel them around a running track faster than they had run before. To be precise, the kids' average running scores in the 50-meter run improved from 8.51 seconds, when the Nike-brand elements were disguised, to 8.09 seconds when the brand elements were visible—an improvement of 0.42 seconds. It may not have been the 20% improvement that I "promised" in my Priming, but it was hugely significant[14] individual improvement in a 50-meter course, and it was real.

That seven-year-old boy back in 1973 wasn't wrong about running faster in elite-brand running shoes. The youngsters in my study did run significantly faster when they were wearing Nikes and *knew* they were wearing Nikes.

But the effect wasn't limited to the runners who believed that the power of the magic swoosh was on their sides. The group who believed that they were *not* wearing Nikes ran significantly slower (8.76 seconds) than they had before they were exposed to my promotional promises (8.49 seconds).

In other words, the Nike spell had not only affected the wearers of the (perceived) product; it had also had a measurable impact on runners who believed that they were *not* wearing the branded product. This demonstrated that the power of the brand was *not* limited to users of the brand; it also negatively affected users who believed they were running in a competing (inferior) brand.

I also reviewed the questionnaires that I asked the kids to complete—the ones that asked how much they expected the Nike-branded shoe to improve their performance and how motivated they were to improve their performance.

Although all the youngsters had read the same brand promises, the ones who believed that they were wearing the Nike-branded shoes both *expected* and *wanted* to improve their performance significantly more than those who wore what they had believed were inferior shoes. In addition, the higher those motivation and expectation scores, the greater the improvement in those runners' performances.

One last portion of the results was left to consider, and here my number crunching brought out another unexpected finding from my study. When we returned to the schools one week later and had the students run the same course again in their own shoes, the students who had previously run while wearing the visibly branded Nikes reverted to their baseline running averages, while the kids who had run in the perceived "knockoff" shoes now ran significantly slower (8.72 seconds) than their pre-experiment baseline times with their own shoes (8.59 seconds).

In other words, kids who thought that they were not running with the coveted Nike shoes in the original test continued to experience poor running performance while running in their own shoes even a week following the original test.

I had my answers: The magic of the brand could, indeed, make youngsters run faster. It could also bewitch them into running more slowly, and the spell could last across time (at least one week).

But these answers created so many more questions: How does the BRAND*cebo* effect work on a physiological basis? What elements are needed to create enhanced physiological effects? And what can we learn from this about the value of branding, itself?

This is what BRAND*cebo is all* about: the real but almost eerie phenomenon that is created at the intersection of brand and placebo that affects consumers' behavior and performance.

Next, we will look at brain science and advertising practices, physiology and psychology, to help us understand how the BRAND*cebo* effect works and why it matters to you as a marketer, a businessperson, and a consumer in today's world of omnipresent promotion.

so many others had miraculously appeared cured. They were deeply motivated to be cured as there was no other medical recourse short of bloodletting and fevered rest.

The popularity of the King's Touch grew phenomenally over the centuries. King Henry IV of France is reputed to have touched 1,500 subjects in one grueling session, while England's Charles II is rumored to have used the royal touch on over 90,000 subjects between 1660 and 1682.

While no scientific data meeting today's standards exists as to the efficacy of their majesties' touch, anecdotal evidence suggests there were some positive effects.

Sergeant-Surgeon, Richard Wiseman, a prominent English surgeon wrote, "I myself have been a frequent eye-witness of many hundreds of cures performed by his majesty's touch alone, without any assistance of chirurgery" (archaic term for surgery) "and those many of them such as had tried out the endeavors of able chirurgeons before they came thither[1]."

King Charles' own surgeon wrote, "... I do humbly presume to assert, that more souls have been healed by his majesty's sacred hand in one year than have ever been cured by all the chirurgeons of his three kingdoms ever since his happy Restoration[2]."

In effect, the concept of faith is the idea of believing in a higher power. Almost every religion (certainly the most common ones) asks its followers to have faith, but for many this places the burden of proof within a belief.

In all faiths, stories of miracles—not magic—are foundational in establishing the validity and eternity of the faith and are contingent upon the unconditional belief of followers. For the believer, every situation in life, trivial or profound, is viewed as an act of God (or a higher power). But one could argue that those miracles sometimes exist because of the belief that these miracles are true "miracles." I know of stories in which women who were previously unable to get pregnant immediately conceived upon receiving a blessing from a priest or rabbi. These women were absolutely convinced that their pregnancies came about because of the blessing they received. Other stories are told of people in terrible car accidents who survive unscathed. They attribute their survival to an outside force.

As we can see, the placebo effect isn't actually new; it's ancient. We're wired for it, mentally and physically, and we've been using it for millennia. The point isn't that these "miracles" didn't happen, but rather that the physical manifestation of the power of the mind is far stronger than we might have thought.

SALINE SOLUTION OR MORPHINE?

In more recent history, and therefore more stringently and scientifically documented, there are a myriad of powerful examples of the mental and physical effects of belief in the placebo. Dr. Henry K. Beecher documented the first such example in 1955 in research on soldiers injured in World War II.

Beecher, a Harvard-trained anesthesiologist, served with the Allied forces in World War II in North Africa and Italy. He tended to wounded soldiers and witnessed the nightmarish conditions of war at the front. During the winters, the weather was wet, cold, and muddy. Soldiers arrived not just torn up by shrapnel from German bombs but also often wet and freezing either from being rained upon or from lying wounded on the wet earth.

In Italy, Beecher witnessed a phenomenon that would change the way we see placebos forever. An anesthesiologist, Beecher was assisted by an Army nurse. When the morphine supply ran dangerously low, Beecher saw how the nurse, in an act of deceitful empathy, assured a wounded soldier that the injection she was giving him was morphine that would relieve his pain immediately. Instead, she gave him a shot of saline solution, which was what was available. To the surprise of both the nurse and Beecher, the soldier's pain was reduced and his condition began to improve[3].

This event so impressed Beecher that when he returned to Harvard, he immediately began to study this phenomenon. Specifically, Beecher wanted to design a system for testing new drugs to ensure their actual efficacy rather than any results that might be attributed to what became known as "the placebo effect."

In 1955 he wrote a paper entitled "The Powerful Placebo[4]" in which he emphasized the need for double-blind, placebo-controlled clinical trials to replace the more haphazard trials of the time. In these trials, he recommended comparing the effectiveness of new drugs against a control group that was administered a "placebo" instead of the drug being tested. Previously, participants were simply given doses of the new medicine and researchers watched and recorded the results.

The placebo-controlled drug trials turned out to be so beneficial that today, the FDA requires any new drug to beat the placebo in at least two clinical trials—a surprisingly difficult task.

IT'S NOT ONLY IN YOUR HEAD

Fabrizio Benedetti is a professor in the Department of Neuroscience at the University of Turin, in Turin, Italy. For years (and at least for the 1990s), Benedetti has been fascinated by the neurological effects of the placebo phenomenon. In his early days of studying the placebo—when it was still relegated "all in your head" status and was anathema in the medical community—he unearthed data from scientists in the United States that claimed the placebo had a neurological basis[4]. Intrigued, Benedetti dug deeper.

It appeared that American researchers had identified a neurological pathway that prevented the placebo from working, thereby providing for greater understanding of its actual functioning. Apparently, quite on its own and without drugs of any sort, the brain reacts to conditions of stress by producing opioids—analgesic compounds that reduce pain, in other words, natural painkillers. A drug called naloxone blocks these natural opioids as well as their synthetic brethren. This finding, the scientific equivalent of a candle shedding dim light, at least illuminated a pathway for Benedetti to begin understanding the neurological underpinnings of the placebo effect.

Over the years, Benedetti's research identified many other facets of our self-healing abilities, which the placebo effect triggers. The same opioids mentioned above also stabilize heart rate and breathing, and can reduce the secretion of cortisol—a common and potentially dangerous byproduct of stress. Additionally, the neuroreceptor dopamine that is released through the placebo effect can improve motor functions in people with Parkinson's disease.

It's only a matter of time before we understand more of how placebos affect us physiologically and facilitate our tapping more deeply into the body's natural healing abilities. However, the point for this book is it works—both physically and mentally.

HOW OTHERS' PERCEPTIONS CAN AFFECT YOUR IQ

The placebo effect isn't just mental; it's deeply physical. The World War II soldiers who received injections of saline instead of morphine had fewer neurons telling them they were in pain. The release of placebo-generated opioids reduced pain and stress. The soldiers experienced less pain because they actually *felt* less pain.

The interconnectedness of mind and body runs deep and is inseparable. As we believe, so we become, and it doesn't stop with opioids and dopamine.

In 1965, researchers Robert Rosenthal and Lenore Jacobson asked a question: Will grade school children who are expected by their teachers to have greater intellectual growth, experience more growth than their classmates for whom no such expectations are set?[5]

To answer this question, the researchers went to an elementary school in California. Each student from grades one through six was given a fake IQ test (the Harvard Test of Inflected Acquisition)[6]. One fifth of the students were chosen at random and identified to the teachers as expected to be "growth spurters" based on the test. The teachers believed that the IQ test had been real and that the results had successfully identified students with the most potential.

At the end of the school year, every student was given another IQ test, disguised yet again. The results? On average, those students who had been expected to perform better by their teachers had greater IQ growth than their control-group counterparts did. While the average for all six grades was a 3.8 IQ point increase, those children in grades one and two did shockingly better. First graders had an average of a 15.4 IQ point increase above the control group while second graders came out 9.5 points ahead.

Why the youngest cohort of the study came out best is the source of much debate: one idea is they might have been more malleable; another possibility is that the teachers didn't already know them and have preset expectations. However, this wasn't just some short-term gain on a random test—almost every child that was expected to do better physically did so with a higher IQ. They came away smarter. Demonstrably so.

An additional phenomenon was at play here as well. The teachers experienced a placebo effect in that they believed certain children were smarter and as a result expected them to perform better. The perception most likely affected the way they treated these kids and overestimated the value they applied to their academic performance. In this sense, the teachers looked at the "smart" kids the way they would a desired brand.

PYGMALION VS. GOLEM

The results of this study were so impressive they became known as the Pygmalion Effect (also known as the Rosenthal Effect and the Observer-Expectancy Effect). The premise being when a leader expects more from you, you perform correspondingly better; you internalize the outer belief. Powerful stuff, yes?

The inverse is known as the Golem Effect (named after a mythical creature that was created with good intentions but became corrupt: It is a metaphor for negative self-fulfilling prophecies), whereby low expectations from an outside source lead to low performance in the individual at the receiving end of that expectation. When considered in the context of minority and disadvantaged children and adults, great social concern should arise from this. If, as a society, we base our expectations by the color of an individual's skin, their ethnicity, or even the way they dress, then what effect are we having on their future? Perhaps it's stronger than we realize. President George W. Bush called this effect "the soft bigotry of low expectations[7]."

THE DNA OF BELIEF

In 2005, Bruce Lipton, a former medical school professor and research scientist, published his groundbreaking research on the interaction of the mind and the body, and how to harness the power of the mind, in a book entitled *The Biology of Belief*[8]. Lipton argues that our biology is not controlled by our DNA and genes; rather, our DNA, and therefore our biology, is controlled by our beliefs, which affect our positive and negative thoughts.

When viewed from this perspective, one wonders just how pervasive placebo effects are within our society. What type of placebo effect(s) are you under, right now, as you sit reading this book? What subtleties might have directed you to one course of action or another: your self-perception whose only truths lay in the strength of your beliefs?

PLACEBO AND VOODOO DEATHS

If this is all true, you ask, then could the power of beliefs and expectations be mobilized for outcomes a person doesn't want?

Well, yes, actually.

"Voodoo Death" is the title of a classic 1942 research paper by physiologist Walter Cannon[9]. In this book, Cannon coins the term "Voodoo Death" to describe the lethal, psychosomatic effects of strong emotional shock, specifically fear: the strong belief of some outside deadly force focused on the victim with the intent to kill can, in some cases, induce the desired response, i.e., death.

Bone pointing by ancient aboriginal witchdoctors in Australia is one such oft-cited example. The witchdoctor points the bone at the victim and utters a curse. If the beliefs are strongly enough held in the society in which this ritual takes place, the victim will die within days or weeks. Knowing what we know about the power of the mind in connection with the body, this comes as an extreme, but not complete surprise.

Australian Bone Pointers[10]

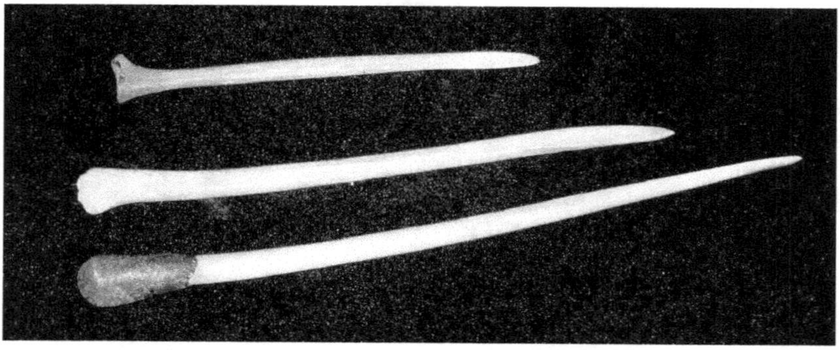

NOW, WHAT IS A PLACEBO?

So what actually is this effect that so permeates our minds and cultures?

According to the American Heritage Dictionary, a Placebo is: "A substance that has positive effects as a result of a patient's perception that it is beneficial rather than as a result of a causative ingredient[11]."

Dr. Ted Kaptchuk, Professor of Medicine at Harvard Medical School, underscores the idea that placebo is not only in our heads: "... Researchers have found that placebo treatments—interventions with no active ingredients—can stimulate real physiological responses, from changes in heart rate and blood pressure to chemical activity in the brain, in cases involving pain, depression, anxiety, fatigue, and even some symptoms of Parkinson's[12]."

Kaptchuk is the Director of the Harvard-wide Program in Placebo Studies and Therapeutic Encounter hosted at Beth Israel Deaconess Medical Center where some of the best and brightest minds in the medical world are joining forces to study the placebo effect in medicine. Kaptchuk said that not including placebo in medical treatment today "is like ignoring a huge chunk of healthcare[13]."

NOCEBO—THE OTHER SIDE OF THE COIN

Where the placebo effect creates a positive outcome, the nocebo effect, Latin for "I shall harm," has the opposite effect.

According to Merriam-Webster Dictionary, the nocebo effect is: "a harmless substance that when taken by or administered to a patient is associated with harmful side effects or worsening of symptoms due to negative expectations or the psychological condition of the patient[14]."

An article in the Smithsonian magazine defines the nocebo effect as "the phenomenon in which inert substances or mere suggestions of substances actually bring about negative effects in a patient or research participant[15]."

As we can see, the placebo effect has a darker side. It's no surprise that the mind-body connection can cause harm as well as good. Look at the deleterious effects of stress. Some studies estimate that 75% of doctor's visits are caused by this factor, alone. So while this book is about the positive side, the placebo effect, I would be remiss not to bring up its ugly cousin, the nocebo effect. By understanding both, we can much more carefully avoid pitfalls and create a positive, mutually beneficial, placebo in branding.

Which brings me to the real topic of this book...

THE PLACEBO EFFECT IN BRANDING

Whether you're a businessperson reading this book to gain a competitive edge, or a curious individual fascinated with the inner workings of the mind, you'd be interested to learn that studies have proven that the placebo effect is just as alive and well in branding as it is in medicine. In fact, it's all around us every day, and has been for most of our lives.

I based my doctoral dissertation on the brand placebo phenomenon and its spillover, the Ricochet Effect. With over 20 years of experience in building and executing brand strategies for companies, I've seen and documented the placebo effect countless times. It's real. It's strong. And it's not just "all in the head." Here are some examples.

RAY-BAN MAKES YOU SEE BETTER, REALLY!

In a 2011 study conducted at the Hebrew University of Jerusalem[16], researchers sought to understand the relationship between a brand's reputation and its actual functionality. Did a stronger brand name (based on brand awareness and brand equity index) mean a better product, or was the brand's reputation enough to create a placebo effect and the real cause of success?

Sixty participants were asked to place their chins on a stable pad 70 centimeters away from a glaringly bright light. They were all given exactly the same sunglasses to reduce glare. Half of the participants received a pair of sunglass bearing the Ray-Ban tag while the other half received sunglasses bearing the name of a relatively unknown inferior brand, Mango. Each participant was presented sequentially with 84 cards displaying unrelated words. Each was told to say the word on each card aloud and as quickly as possible. In fact, they were given a financial incentive to say the words as quickly as they could and without errors.

Results showed that here, too, the placebo effect was in play. Ray-Ban wearers made, on average, 6.2 errors while Mango wearers averaged 12.2 errors; that's twice as many mistakes while wearing the exact same sunglasses. But it doesn't stop there.

Ray-Ban wearers were also significantly faster, completing the task in 64.4 seconds versus 102.8 seconds for their Mango counterparts. Clearly, the Ray-Ban wearers didn't need to slow down to achieve better results. They were significantly faster and more accurate, yet wore the same physical sunglasses as the slower, more inaccurate group[17]. Ray-Ban's reputation was enough to create a stronger performance in its wearers, a placebo effect quite similar to pain-reducing saline solution that was as effective as real morphine.

COKE OR PEPSI? ASK YOUR BRAIN

While the study of mind and body and the interaction between them has captured the interest of researchers for centuries, there have been technological advancements over the past few decades, such as functional Magnetic Resonance Imaging (fMRI). Here is how it works: when there's increased activity in one area of the brain, that area requires more blood flow to supply the necessary glucose and oxygen—the fuel, and the fuel "burner." Magnetic fields are able to pick up the changes in blood flow that show up on images.

fMRI image (circles denote areas of increased activity)[18]

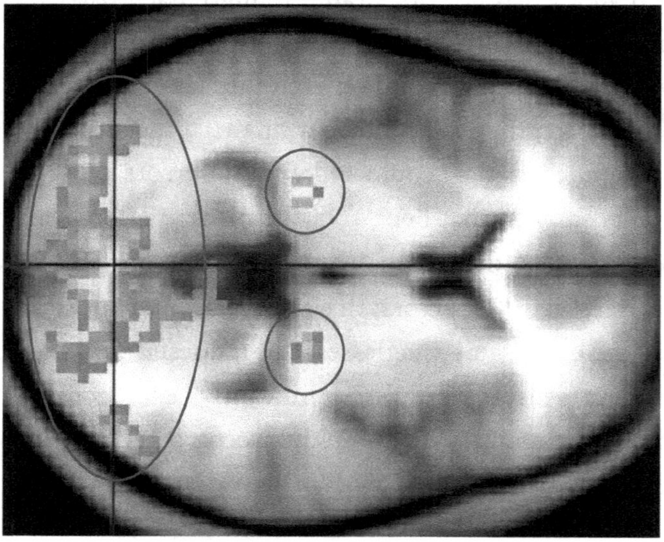

The use of fMRI has enabled a shift in research approaches. Now we can focus more on the unity and interdependency of the mind-body relationship. Several recent studies have validated the scientific qualities of human beliefs as triggers to physiological reactions.

In an interesting study utilizing fMRI[19], participants were given two cola drinks: one Coke, the other Pepsi. Researchers chose these two drinks because consumers often have strong opinions as to which they prefer (despite the fact that they're nearly identical in makeup and taste).

The test was conducted in two phases. In the first phase, the drinks were delivered in unmarked cups; the volunteers didn't know which brand they received. In this scenario, preference was equally split between the two brands with half preferring one anonymous drink and the other half preferring the other.

In the second phase of the test, when participants were told the brand name of the cola drinks they received, they consistently preferred Coke over Pepsi. The fMRI images showed that Coke actually lit up the memory-related areas of the brain, which the researchers attributed to the brand's deep-seated cultural influences that drive the choice. Pepsi drinkers did not demonstrate this same physical response.

However—and this is where it gets interesting—researchers also went so far as to lie to the participants as to which drink they were tasting: Coke drinkers were told they were given Pepsi, and vice versa. Yet regardless of which drink they actually consumed, the brain 'reacted' (in fMRI images) only when it *thought* they were drinking Coke.

The researchers concluded: "There are visual images and marketing messages that have insinuated themselves into the nervous systems of humans that consume drinks[20]." Coca-Cola had achieved this level of branding; Pepsi has not.

Deep stuff, literally. This isn't to say we aren't all smart consumers; it's that the power of our perceptions has enormous physiological influence over the product experience.

WHY DO EXPENSIVE PRODUCTS PERFORM BETTER?

"Well, you get what you pay for." You must have heard this phrase before. Think of your perception, in terms of quality, of a $1.99 bottle of wine versus a $150 one. Quite different, isn't it?

Baba Shiv, Ziv Carmon, and Dan Ariely, three distinguished researchers in the field of decision making, were curious about whether or not an individual's belief surrounding the price and, therefore, value of a product affected them physiologically. Would an expensive product 'work' better? Here's how their study worked:

Individuals who exercised regularly at a fitness center were presented with an energy drink[21]. They were given a list of the drink's ingredients and told that the specific batch they would consume was the most recent. Half of the participants were told that the drink cost $2.89, while the other half was informed that the drink actually cost $2.89, but as a result of a huge volume purchase, was discounted to $2.00 ($0.89 off). The individuals were then asked to consume their energy drinks—one before and one after their workouts.

Participants who consumed the "discounted" energy drink reported a significantly lower workout intensity and correspondingly higher fatigue than their counterparts who consumed the full-priced version. Evidently, participants attributed different quality traits based exclusively on price. It would appear that there had been a subconscious negative assessment that was applied to the discounted product, which resulted in a placebo effect.

SO, WHAT'S IN A PLACEBO?

As we can tell, the placebo effect occurs in more than just the medical aspects of our lives, and is a powerfully effective force. Undoubtedly, we've all been under its spell without even knowing it, and most likely still are so today. Part of the reason we have such strong emotional ties to brands is directly attributable to the placebo effect.

So how does it actually work? Are there specific steps or elements that are needed to put it into effect? How can this information be used for branding with the best of intentions for all parties concerned?

Studies, including my own, have shown that three ingredients bring forth the placebo effect with the greatest potency: Priming, Expectation, and Desire.

In Chapters 4, 5, and 6, I explain in detail each of these elements, how they relate to each other, and how they can be implemented within marketing and branding. In other words, how Priming + Expectation + Desire = BRAND*cebo*!

In the next chapter, I'll approach the placebo from a different angle, one that considers our emotions and personal loyalties as deeply as we would experience them in an intimate relationship.

Chapter 3

Romancing the Brand: How to Turn Brand Consumers into Brand Lovers

The first step on the road to BRAND*cebo* is understanding that brands are relationships. Over the last quarter century, this statement has become a truism. Brands aren't, in fact, casual associations; they can be strong relationships—relationships that change lives.

The rock band The Grateful Dead developed their brand throughout the '60s until, by the '70s, their loyal Deadhead "customers" were following them around the country in a perpetual pilgrimage that reorganized their lives, values, spirituality, and livelihoods. Deadheads don't just "like" Jerry Garcia and his band; rather their influence has run so deep it has imprinted itself upon generations of music lovers, musicians, and aspects of our very culture. Children have been named after the band members, the music and lyrics have influenced countless other bands, and legends have been built on this brand of musicians.

In the same vein, the Harley-Davidson brand has developed, over the last 30 years, into a total lifestyle commitment through sponsored events, owners' clubs, and tie-in merchandising. Harley owners talk about their rides as if they're family. The relationship has gone far beyond that of a machine and a person; Harley riders are committed to their brand from the depth of their beings.

Sports fans are certainly caught up in the euphoria and heartbreak of their favorite teams' wins and losses. People will travel around the world to watch them. And on game night, there's no option other than to sit and witness the unfolding of their favorite team's (read *brand's*) skill and sportsmanship. When they win, fans feel vindicated; they were right all along to love this team. When the team loses, extreme disappointment and even depression may set in. A recent study has even found that fans of losing teams are more prone to weight gain, much as people are in the aftermath of a romantic breakup[1].

But in what way are these ephemeral concepts that we call "brands" similar to the states of emotional connectedness that we call "relationships?" As we explore the placebo effect in later chapters, we will learn that a brand's power is modulated by the relationship that surrounds it, so let's begin by understanding exactly what I mean when I say, "Brand Romance."

FOURNIER'S SEVEN CHARACTERISTICS

Susan Fournier, founder of the brand relationships sub-field in marketing, has spent years exploring this subject[2]. She's identified seven characteristics of human relationships that are also manifested in brand relationships. Some of them are quite startling.

Viewing branding and relationships in this light, we can learn how to deepen our branding relationships and increase the likelihood that we can evoke placebo effects that will be mutually beneficial to consumers and the businesses that serve them.

The seven characteristics Fournier has identified are:

1. Behavioral Interdependence
2. Personal Commitment
3. Love and Passion
4. Nostalgic Connection
5. Self-Concept Connection
6. Intimacy
7. Perceived Quality

Let's explore each characteristic:

1. BEHAVIORAL INTERDEPENDENCE

In a good relationship, actions of the partners are intertwined. The behavior of one influences, and is influenced by, the actions of the other. People respond to each other. The two parties need each other, are important to each other, and depend upon each other.

Consider a marriage. One person voices some need or dissatisfaction. "I really need us to stick to the family budget we agreed to." If the other person is responsive, the partners like what they get, and the marriage gains in value. Because of its value, when the going gets tough, the partners are likely to seek solutions that will help them preserve the relationship. The marriage is likely to continue.

On the other hand, if one or both partners chronically fails to respond to the other partner's need, or responds in a negative way, the marriage loses value and the relationship deteriorates.

It is much the same with brands. Businesses direct actions and communications to their customers. Customers aim actions and communications back to businesses. Those volleys of behavior can be as mutually responsive as a waltz; customers may buy in response to promotions and new product introductions, while companies may tailor their services and products to what they learn from their clients through sales numbers and feedback. They continually shape their work to better fit the customer's needs. But if the volleys are not mutually responsive, if the parties are simply shouting at each other without listening, the relationship falls apart and the customer walks away.

2. PERSONAL COMMITMENT

In a good relationship, partners are committed to each other. They have an agreement, whether verbal or not, to stand by each other. The accumulated experience of interdependence has added so much value to each party that when difficulties come, the two stay together and work things out. They are loyal to each other.

Consider, similarly, a good, committed employee/boss relationship. The employee values what they get from the arrangement: a career, a paycheck, loyalty, mentoring, structure, and hopefully success. The employer also values what they get: efficiency, effectiveness, loyalty, and compliance to direction. These benefits motivate each party to be committed to the relationship. They carry enough weight that when the relationship is tested—say by a mistake or an argument— the two parties find the inner resources to veer away from the ease of a pink slip or an angry resignation and work towards a solution and a way to continue the relationship.

In the same sense, when a customer is committed to a brand, they value it enough to stick with it even through challenging times.

For example, when Southwest Airlines first launched in Texas in the early 1970s, this innovative, young airline demonstrated a commitment to cheap airfares. It provided direct, always-on-time flights in the Dallas-Houston-San Antonio triangle for an astonishing $26 per regular ticket. At this price point, the company quickly became extremely successful and popular among business travelers.

However, in an attempt to take out the scrappy new kid on the block, its larger, more established competitor, Braniff, cut its regular fare to $13, a price that Southwest could not match and remain in business. But instead of abandoning their commitment to discount fares, Southwest ran a full-page ad in the *Dallas Morning News* that called upon its customers to help keep the airline "in the air," so to speak. Southwest explained that it could match Braniff's $13 rate with the caveat that this would cause the company to file for bankruptcy within three months. This would leave the market to Braniff, which could raise its price at any point and to any level.

If, however, loyal customers supported Southwest Airlines by opting to pay the full $26 fare, they would receive a free bottle of premium liquor as a token of the company's appreciation. Most importantly, this would allow the young airline to survive. Eighty percent of the company's customers opted in and paid double the price of its competition[3].

In spite of heavy pressure, Southwest stayed faithful to its customers and their need for low-cost, in-state travel. And in return, its customers stayed faithful to the company. Southwest's actions not only allowed the airline to survive but also made it, for a time, the largest distributor of Chivas, Crown Royal, and Smirnoff in Texas.

Now that's a beautiful story of brand loyalty.

3. LOVE AND PASSION

Think for a moment about a satisfying romantic relationship. The partners want to spend all their time with each other. They dislike being apart, an intense emotional bond holds them together, and they often and publicly demonstrate their connection. That's love and passion.

That's also the feeling of the guitarist who won't even consider buying any guitar except a Martin. It's the same feeling held by a craft beer aficionado who hotly debates the merits of different brands for hours on end with fellow zealots. That's the feeling of the Coke drinker who laughs in the face of a hapless server who dares to offer a Pepsi. That Coke drinker would rather go dry than drink something that is very nearly identical to Coke in every way except brand. That's love and passion.

Like any good relationship, the passion must go both ways. Brands must also be passionate about their customers. They must study them, communicate with them, court them, treasure them, and put them at the center of all of their company's activities.

Businesses like Southwest Airlines, Apple, Nordstrom, and Whole Foods have learned that love and passion must be reciprocal for the virtuous cycle of mutual fulfillment of needs to establish itself.

There is also a dark side to passion, however, when a partner falls out of favor. We see this with bitter divorces and with brands.

For example, consumer satisfaction with airlines has deeply deteriorated, and many brand relationships have turned sour. (Think, for a moment, about the video of United Airlines employees dragging a customer down the aisle and off the plane. This not only hurt the poor passenger, but also deeply upset other loyal United customers.) Overworked and underpaid staff, extra charges for luggage and food, and little recourse for wrongs, such as flight cancellations without notice or lost bags, have all become part of the everyday travel experience. Not surprisingly, customers have a distinctive bitterness towards and cynicism about an airline's performance, which in some cases approaches loathing.

4. NOSTALGIC CONNECTION

In long-term relationships, interactions are not simply moments in the here and now; they are also weighted with associations accumulated through experiences. Memories and emotions rise from the past to color the present, for good or ill.

Take, for example, the relationship between adult siblings. As they've grown up and found their own divergent paths in the world, brothers and sisters still share a lifelong history of experiences unique to them. Similar experiences in the present are likely to trigger these memories: the smell of their mother's home-cooked casseroles, the sound of a train passing in the night, or maybe even the local accent and slang that, over the years, has faded in their own words and styles. These experiences may be flavored by a dominant emotional state—pride, fun, fear, rivalry, protectiveness, or anger—that causes the trigger and the emotion to feel connected.

Successful companies make room for a nostalgic connection in their brand relationships. Scenery, music, cars, and movies from when the target demographic was young are famously potent for capturing the heart of a generation. Connecting with anything that makes a consumer feel good is always a smart idea for a marketer.

For example, consider how, riding a wave of 1970s nostalgia, Eggo Waffles revisited its own memorable "L'eggo my Eggo" campaign. Their new ads in 2014 harkened back to the old slogan while updating it for the digital age with images of a family texting the familiar slogan to each other at the breakfast table. When the nostalgia factor is strong, it enhances loyalty and passion, carries an implicit message of long-term staying power and authenticity, and makes consumers more willing to spend[4].

5. SELF-CONCEPT CONNECTION

Partners in deep and long-lasting relationships often share common interests, activities, and opinions. They support and affirm each other in these areas, areas that ultimately become defining facets of identity and self-concept.

Take, for instance, best friends. They have probably chosen each other because they share common interests that they can talk about and explore together, which increase the value of the relationship. Doing things together yields a bank of joint experiences and memories that further cement the bond. Shared opinions confirm each person's understanding of the world—"I must be right because you believe the same thing"—and remove the anxiety of opinion challenges from the relationship. This creates a reassuring atmosphere of mutual affirmation.

Analogously, brands have "personalities," and when the brand personality is congruent with the consumer's self-image, brand loyalty and satisfaction increase[5]. In fact, this is the ultimate goal of branding: to go beyond the level of simply associating a brand with being "cool" to actually feeling better about yourself as a person to realizing a higher level of self-actualization because of the love of a brand. This is the highest and truest form of brand romance.

To make this magic happen, corporations can invest in marketing that gives their target demographic that comforting feeling of reflected self-image. As the viewer loves their self-image, therefore they also love the brand.

For example, does a business advertise at NASCAR events or in the back pages of *The New Yorker*? Does it offer its message through an edgy, postmodern style or a more classic approach? What ethnic groups are reflected in these ads? All are significantly different reflections of self-image.

These are all decisions that go directly to the heart of what kind of self-concept connection a company is trying to make with its consumers. Many of the choices are made not only to *reflect* their customer's self-concept but also to *shape* it. Companies want to make their customers feel hip, young, elegant, earthy, athletic, like a good ole boy or whatever the desired identity may be. When your brand connects to the customer's self-definition, the customer wants more of your product or service.

6. INTIMACY

In a successful relationship, a profound understanding exists between partners. They know each other at a deep level. They've asked questions and listened to the answers. They've witnessed each other's responses to the experiences their common interests have caused them to share. Each knows what the other likes and doesn't like. Each is rich in information about the other.

Consider a healthy parent-child relationship. From the day the baby comes home from the hospital, attentive parents are gathering data about what soothes that child, what stimulates them, what they need, what they hate. At the same time, the baby is gathering information about how to make life work with that particular set of parents: what sounds and movements will result in a diaper being changed or food being presented, what sensations predict being left alone, which parental voice tones go along with gentle holding and which go along with rough handling. Intimacy is created by information received and given.

In a similar way, brand relationships are infused with information. The passionate Mustang driver can quote technical details on the horsepower, number of cylinders, engine displacement, zero-to-sixty performance, torque, and so forth of the beloved car. If given the opportunity, that driver will also inundate you with details about the history of the model and the company that made it.

This deep understanding of a product that a passionate consumer develops is then mirrored by the deep understanding of their customers that a passionate company develops. That company is interested in getting as much information as possible about the people who use their products or services, and will devise complex methods of intelligence to gather it.

For example, every time a buyer swipes a credit card at the grocery store, the purchase data is immediately transmitted to the store, and a discount coupon appears on the receipt—a coupon calculated to appeal to that specific shopper based on their past purchasing history. Some stores, like Walmart, even use video to track customers' movement in the store in order to identify strolling tendencies and, over time, organize merchandise accordingly. Interests, age, socioeconomic class, gender, geographic location, political leanings, needs, likes, dislikes—all of these are of burning interest to the company that wants their brand relationship with the consumer to be an intimate one.

7. PERCEIVED QUALITY

In a satisfying and long-lasting relationship, each partner believes the other is high quality and the best possible choice. They assume the performance and attitudes of each side are excellent. Each partner has a high opinion of the other, and assumes the other has a high opinion of them.

Consider a good business partnership. Both partners feel that the other is good at what they do and that they add value to the relationship. They have, after all, chosen each other, and the belief that their collaborator is top-notch is reassuring and confirms that the choice they made was an intelligent one. It feels good to know that a partner will have your back. It also feels good to be right about whom you've chosen to take that role.

Brand relationships have this same dimension of high mutual regard. The customer believes they have chosen the best out of all the available alternatives. They want to believe this because confirming it means they've made a smart choice. In an excellent brand relationship, they also believe that the company appreciates them and treats them like a valued customer. And in a truly excellent brand relationship, the company actually does.

With the American Express Platinum card, customers are willing to pay a $400 annual fee to obtain the same benefits that other credit cards offer at no charge. Why? Because American Express treats them like members of an elite club with exclusive access to luxurious airport lounges and the bimonthly, high-end, aspiration-filled *Departure* magazine. American Express is doing everything possible to make its customers feel special, and customers reciprocate by attributing high quality to the brand and choosing it for their credit needs.

The "romance" customers feel for the card goes far beyond its utilitarian use. The superego is stimulated by the branding, which echoes back to the customer's self-image and highest form of self-actualization. All this occurs despite the fact the Amex card is still not honored by many retailers around the world.

BRANDS AS RELATIONSHIPS

Fournier's work has gone a long way towards demonstrating that when we say, "Brands are relationships," we are not talking in vague generalities. Rather, she has identified specific dimensions of behavior and attitude that are common to both what we conventionally call "relationships" and what we call "brands."

In the following chapters, I explain the placebo effect in the world at large and in branding in particular. Within this explanation, you will recognize Fournier's brand-relationship characteristics and develop yet a deeper understanding of and relationship to branding.

Chapter 4

Priming: Of Mice, Men, and Soda Pop

How to Make Customers Believe What You Want Them to Believe

As a child growing up in Jerusalem, I was passionate about one thing above all else: soccer. I lived and breathed the sport, and I still love it today.

Back then, I played in the neighborhood games and was always considered good; not great, but good. That is, until one day when an older kid, one who we respected and who coached us from time to time, said to me, "You play just like Johan Cruyff."

For those of you who aren't rabid soccer fans, Cruyff was the Dutch player who, in the 1970's, was soccer's equivalent to God . He was the Michael Jordan, Roger Federer, or Tiger Woods of his time. And this older kid told me, in front of other players, that I played just like him.

Johan Cruyff[1]

You couldn't have said anything more impactful, and from that day on, I played better soccer than I ever had before. I thought about Cruyff when I played and considered what he would do. How would he handle this pass? When would he kick? What would I look like in the orange and white colors of Holland? I even emulated his body language.

Over the course of that year, my game improved dramatically. I'd never considered trying out for the youth team of Beitar Yerushalayim, Jerusalem's prominent soccer club, but that year I decided to do it, and I made the team.

Fast forward to high school. The coach there changed my position from midfielder to sweeper. But Cruyff didn't play sweeper, so my association with him diminished and my game deteriorated.

I said to the coach, "I play midfield. Why do you want me to be a sweeper?"

He replied, "You play sweeper so well, you remind me of Beckenbauer."

Franz Beckenbauer, nicknamed Der Kaiser (the King), is still regarded as one of the greatest players of all time—and he played sweeper for his German team. Once again, just by associating my play with his, my game improved.

Franz Beckenbauer [2]

Interestingly, after our opponents heard what I was being called, they started losing more balls to me. My skills hadn't changed and their skills hadn't changed; none of us had been given extra training or coaching. We were the same kids playing the same game, but as my playing improved, theirs deteriorated.

As you can see, many similarities exist between my childhood experiences with soccer and the findings of my dissertation studies many years later. I am still fascinated by what actually happened all those years ago. Why did a bit of flattery affect me so much, and why did it have the opposite effect on my opponents? In hindsight, I know that I was conditioned, or Primed, to believe that I was a better player by being compared to a legendary player. People, including myself, Expected me to play better if I was being compared to a soccer legend. And my Desire to be a better player went through the roof.

PRIMING + EXPECTATION + DESIRE = PLACEBO

Included in this experience was an interesting phenomenon that I also observed in my Nike placebo studies. My opponents responded to their Priming and Expectation of my playing skill by playing correspondingly worse, themselves.

The placebo effect doesn't just occur in sports; it happens every single day in our lives: in disguised IQ tests, medical studies, soccer, and the world of branding. In this chapter, I'll discuss the first essential element in the placebo effect equation: Priming—how it's created and why it works.

Much of the Priming that influences us has nothing to do with the rational mind. It's not like we're pondering long and hard over a spreadsheet full of data in order to learn how Priming occurs at a deep level within the brain; it is so deep that we tap into non-thinking reactions.

Let's sit back, have a Coke, and consider how this happens.

WHAT'S IN A TASTE?

In Chapter 2, I described an important neurological study on taste preferences between Coke and Pepsi drinkers. The study's findings not only shed light on the Coke vs. Pepsi fuss, but they also demonstrate a classic example of the placebo effect in action.

Coke and Pepsi are nearly identical, in that they're composed of water, sugar, a mild stimulant, and flavoring. The similarity is so strong that without their labels, tasters' preferences in the study were even: half preferred Pepsi, and half preferred Coke.

However, when labels were attached to the beverages, tasters consistently preferred Coke. This occurred even when the drinks were *falsely* labeled. In other words, taste didn't matter nearly as much as the belief in which drink they tasted.

How could this possibly be?

PEERING INTO THE BRAIN

Researchers turned to science for answers—specifically, fMRI (functional Magnetic Resonance Imaging), which measures blood flow in the brain.

Given this ability to virtually peel open the brain and look inside, researchers were able to compare the differences in brain activity when conducting blind tasting and brand tasting. The results regarding the cultural impact of brands were nothing short of astounding.

When study participants were told what they were drinking (whether it was the truth or not), a dramatic difference appeared in fMRI images depending on whether the drink was Coke or Pepsi. Coke lit up both the dorsolateral prefrontal cortex and the hippocampus—brain areas that scientists believe affect behavior based on emotions. Specifically, they wrote, "... The hippocampus may participate in recalling cultural information that biases preference judgments[3]."

The Limbic System[4]

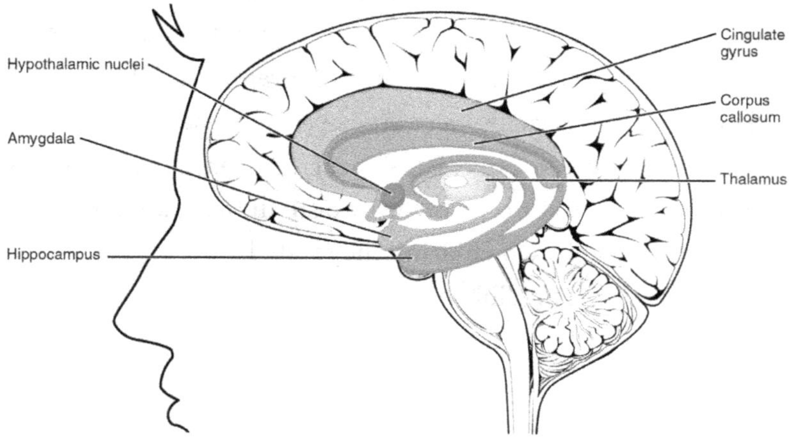

The scientists went on to stipulate that the dorsolateral prefrontal cortex is used when tasting, and the hippocampus is used when accessing layers of cultural influences. Coke triggered increased activity in both areas. Pepsi, on the other hand, had little to no influence on the "cultural" part of the brain.

Given the brazen similarity between the two brands based on taste, why did participants consistently favor Coke? Why did participants' brains "light up" (indicating increased blood flow or activity) in areas that Pepsi didn't?

To understand the answer, we have to visit a rat, and then a dog.

WHAT CAN WE LEARN FROM RATS?

In earlier chapters, I discussed our increasing understanding of and belief in the mind-body connection. As we believe, so we are. Making this point dramatically, the participants in the aforementioned Coke/Pepsi study experienced different physiological effects when they believed they tasted a specific brand. The link between the belief and the body was real and measurable. The formula of the two drinks was not different enough to cause this change, but the *belief* in what they were drinking was.

In 1975, researchers Robert Ader and Nicholas Cohen conducted a relatively simple experiment and in so doing, accidently changed our understanding of the mind-body connection forever[5].

The two scientists were using sweetened water to study taste aversion in rats (as brainiac scientists tend to do on a rainy weekend). The control group of rats was given the sweetened water while the other group received the identically sweetened water but were also injected with a stomachache-causing drug—nothing serious, but uncomfortable. Not surprisingly, the group of rats that got stomachaches stopped drinking the water that they associated with their distress. However, to abide by the study's design, the researchers needed the rats to keep drinking the sweetened water, so they force fed them with eyedroppers. This continued for a while, until some of those rats started dying.

In trying to unravel the mysterious rat deaths, Ader and Cohen noted that the stomachache-inducing drug they'd used was Cytoxan, which also suppresses the immune system. The drug dosage, itself, wasn't lethal, but something else about it was.

Through the injection of Cytoxan combined with regular

intake of the sweetened water, the rats' bodies developed an association between the taste of the sugar water and the drug's effect—the suppression of their immune system. The dead rats had developed viral and bacterial infections that they weren't able to fend off with their lowered immune systems even after they'd stopped being given Cytoxan, and they died of those infections. Additional studies corroborated the event, and it became a landmark study in the placebo effect[6].

Eric Caine, Chairman of the Department of Psychiatry at the University of Rochester Medical Center, said, "Bob Ader and his colleagues transformed the way that we think about the relationship between life events and our environment, and how our bodies respond biologically. His work has extraordinary implications, not only for understanding immunological responses to stress and disease, but also for appreciating the potentially powerful positive effects of what so many call the 'placebo effect[7].'"

Remember that we're talking about rats here. The association that they experienced between drinking sweetened water and lowered immune system performance produced measurable, physiological effects. Unless these were the most brilliant rats in the world, rational thinking didn't enter into it.

Priming doesn't stop with rats; it works in humans, too. A well-known study by John Bargh[8], the social psychologist of Yale University, demonstrated how smart college students can be primed with word associations.

The college students were divided into two groups. Participants in each group were given sets of five words and were asked to use them to formulate four-word sentences. Easy enough, right? But here's the twist; one group was given words associated with elderly stereotypes, such as worried, Florida, old, grey, retired, bingo, wrinkle, etc., while the other, the control group, was given neutral words not related to age.

After formulating the requested number of sentences, the students were asked to walk down the hallway to another room, about 32 feet away. Amazingly, those students who had formulated sentences with the elderly-related words walked significantly slower (8.28 seconds) than the students working with more neutral words (7.30 seconds).

This is called *Priming*, a critical element for placebo effect. Conscious, logical thinking wasn't involved; the pace in which the students walk was generated subconsciously in the more ancient midbrain region.

In my own office in San Diego, I use a form of Priming. My office sits at the end of a hallway, and anyone walking down that hallway can easily see the word "YES" on my wall in 2' × 3'-tall red letters. Without a doubt, that sign makes people—including me—feel more positive and uplifted as we enter the office.

A BIT OF TERMINOLOGY

Classical Conditioning is a powerful form of Priming that occurs in the subconscious mind without rational thought, and that is why it is important in this book. The differences between the two, however, are important enough to understand.

Classical Conditioning is a learning process, whereas Priming is a matter of association. Ader's rats had an innate desire to drink water, but through the pairing of the powerful stimulus of Cytoxan with their water, their bodies adapted to the subclinical dose of Cytoxan and lowered the effectiveness of their immune systems even when Cytoxan was no longer administered with the sweet water. That is classical conditioning

The college students, on the other hand, associated the words they were given with a certain lifestyle. This manifested in the way they walked down the hallway. Their bodies didn't 'learn' to walk differently but their subconscious minds responded to the types of words they were given. That is priming.

Subtle but quite distinct. Both are relevant as Priming factors in the placebo effect and, therefore, within branding and BRAND*cebo*.

PAVLOV'S DOGS AND CLASSICAL CONDITIONING

Interestingly, Classical Conditioning, like Ader's placebo-affected rats, was discovered accidently, yet is now one of the most famous scientific studies of all time. Let's look more deeply at the elements involved in Classical Conditioning.

In the late 19th century, a Russian physiologist named Ivan Pavlov was studying the connection between dogs being fed and their salivation—a reliable indicator of expectation of being fed, as any dog owner knows. The original premise was that no one "taught" the dogs to salivate; they did so automatically when presented with food. It was an innate response.

The accidental discovery occurred when Pavlov noticed that, after a while, all it took to get the dogs salivating was him walking in the room, whether he was there to feed them or not. This so affected him that it changed the course of his studies, and history, forever.

Pavlov studied this phenomenon further and discovered several distinct elements of Classical Conditioning.

Classical Conditioning[9]

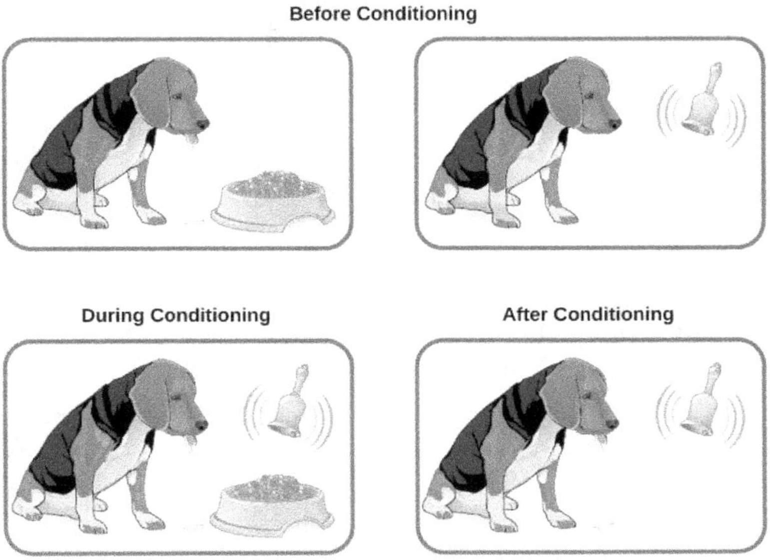

Pavlov formulated an experiment. He already had an unconditioned response from the dogs in the form of salivation when food (an unconditioned stimulus) was brought into the room. No one taught the dogs to salivate in the presence of food; it was innate.

Next, he introduced an unconditioned stimulus to the experiment in the form of a ringing bell before the dogs were fed: A bell was rung and then they were fed. The bell, alone, didn't cause a dog to salivate. The dogs only salivated when they were presented with food, which is a response as hardwired as chasing rabbits or licking their... Well, you know.

However as Pavlov began ringing a bell whenever he brought in food for the dogs, over time they learned to associate the ringing of a bell with being fed. In response, they salivated as soon as they heard the bell, even when food was not immediately present. The unconditioned stimulus became a conditioned stimulus, which led to a conditioned response: salivation. This is Classical Conditioning, and I will show you how it works in branding much as it works with Fido.

As with Ader's rats, Pavlov's dogs weren't intellectual beings. Their response wasn't a rational process or the result of critical thought, or any thought at all. The response was unconscious and physiological.

These studies underscore that the mind-body connection isn't a theory: It's real, measurable, and occurs within us all the time.

COCA-COLA AND TATTOOED BRAINS

So, what do Ader's rats and Pavlov's dogs have to do with Coke, Pepsi, and branding? How did Coca-Cola build such a strong brand that if participants believed that they were drinking Coke, they loved whatever was in their cup, even if it was not Coke?

The clue came in the fMRI results and the structures of the brain that lit up when the Coca-Cola brand was invoked (as opposed to in the "tasting" parts of the brain). Coke accomplished this by the use, intentional or not, of Classical Conditioning, which we now understand better because of Ader and Pavlov's work.

Through effective advertising campaigns, Coca-Cola virtually 'tattooed' the Coke brand into our brains, immediately aligning it with images, text, and music: unconditioned stimuli to which we all have strong, unconditioned, positive responses. By excessively repeating these unconditioned stimuli in connection with their brand, Coke products and logos became conditioned stimuli and evoked a conditioned response, just like Pavlov's bell. Now when we see the Coke logo, we become thirsty. We want a Coke and believe it tastes better than the competitor's soft drink. We have been Primed.

In marketing, we consciously recognize that advertisements serve to tell us about the positive aspects of a product. For example, a car manufacturer may claim that their new model has better cornering capability, the latest safety features, and a faster 0-60 acceleration time. It is these qualities that our conscious mind believes that lead to our buying decisions.

However, a lot more is happening at a deeper level. Experienced marketers know that pairing their product with other unrelated objects and experiences that we feel positive about will make us feel positive about their brand, as well.

For example, a car manufacturer might show a car cruising along a majestic mountain road, with a blue sky above and green fields below. Driving the car might be a handsome, fit man with a beautiful woman as his passenger. These elements are easy to feel good about, and the advertisement experience is overall positive. The car manufacturer proceeds to deliver this positive experience with unrelated positive elements over and over and over again. Our decision-making factory now includes subconscious elements based on that positive association. It's what Coke has been doing so well for so long.

Tennis player Roger Federer is considered one of the most talented athletes in the world and, arguably, the best tennis player of all time. Rolex® presumably pays him a small fortune to wear and advertise their watches. As his image is prominently depicted in ads in which he wears a Rolex, viewers begin to associate superiority, excellence, power, and sex appeal with the watch and, therefore, with themselves—if they wear a Rolex. The Rolex watch is the unconditioned stimulus; the image of Federer wearing the watch is a conditioned stimulus, which leads to the conditioned response: the viewer's feelings of superiority, power, and sex appeal.

The brand reflects the self-image of Rolex's target market, even if it's only the self-image to which they aspire.

This type of Priming has worked so well for Coca-Cola and helped make their success so ubiquitous that in 2012, Coca-Cola estimated that the average annual per capita consumption of Coke (8-fluid ounce) products worldwide was 94. In the United States, that number was a whopping 403[10].

In 2016, the brand, alone, had retail sales of nearly $42 billion, and reached a total brand value of $73.1 billion[11]. To put this in perspective, Pepsi, Budweiser, Starbucks, and Red Bull brands combined are worth only a puny $50 billion. Coke's saturation is such that their logo is estimated to be recognized by 94% of the entire population of the planet. And Coca-Cola claims its name is the second most understood word in the world behind the word "okay[12]." That's big.

However, Coca-Cola's $4 billion worldwide advertising[13] isn't just omnipresent—it's targeted. It aims for our strongest associations, like happiness, family, and community. It also taps into what Fournier called the nostalgic connection[14]. Their ads, which have been around for our entire lifetimes, can remind us of places, events, and special people that have affected our lives.

When you read the lyrics, "I'd like to teach the world to sing in perfect harmony...[15]," how many of you start singing along with that famous jingle? (Or worse—will have the song stuck in your head all day long?) That iconic advertisement presented a multi-racial, multi-gender, and multi-generational group of singers singing about peace on a hilltop, with each singer clutching a bottle of Coke.

The song begins with, "I'd like to build the world a home, and furnish it with love[16]." Later, as we're grooving right along, we hear, "I'd like to buy the world a Coke and keep it company[17]."

The messaging hits us right in our home, values, and community spots and we've been absorbing this same style of advertising for generations.

But they don't stop with home and family. The Coke message is deeply associated with another primal state: thirst. Coke places its brand next to sweating, post-workout people who reek of thirst (unconditioned stimuli), thereby associating the brand with health, fitness, and most importantly, being thirsty. As they do this repeatedly, it becomes a conditioned stimulus. The result, then, is a conditioned response to seeing a Coke ad with actual thirst.

RESISTANCE IS FUTILE

As with Ader's rats and Pavlov's dogs, the Coke/Pepsi taste comparison shows actual physiological changes in the brain. The fMRIs proved increased activity in certain areas of the brain—specifically those thought to do with cultural memories and influence.

Priming has nothing to do with rational, conscious thought. Coca-Cola's staggering advertising budget isn't spilling out information about how Coke is better, healthier, more effective, safer, or even higher quality than other soft drinks. Instead, it positions the Coca-Cola brand name adjacent to images, words, people, and music to deliver its message. They hit our emotions—one of the most powerful drivers of human action.

Much as with Coke ads, watch wearers aren't going to change their entire physique and appearance by strapping on a Rolex. But their subconscious and deeply emotional attachment to this image causes them to purchase the Rolex, anyway. Logically, a compliment and comparison from a soccer coach should not have caused me to become a much better player without additional training, but my emotional and subconscious drive to do so surpassed the power of my conscious mind.

It doesn't even matter if we're paying attention to a conditioned stimulus or not: We don't have to consciously condone or even understand advertising. The mere repetition of Coke paired with positive images predisposes us to seek out Coke products. Try as we might, unless we truly are hermits living in dark caves, we cannot escape the effect of Coke's advertising, which surrounds us on billboards, TV, radio, magazines, arena signs—everywhere.

Our conditioned response to the Coca-Cola brand shows up in our preference for the drink over other drinks even when we only *think* we're drinking it. This is the placebo effect at work, this time in branding.

BUILDING BRAND*cebo*
Step 1: From Awareness to Priming

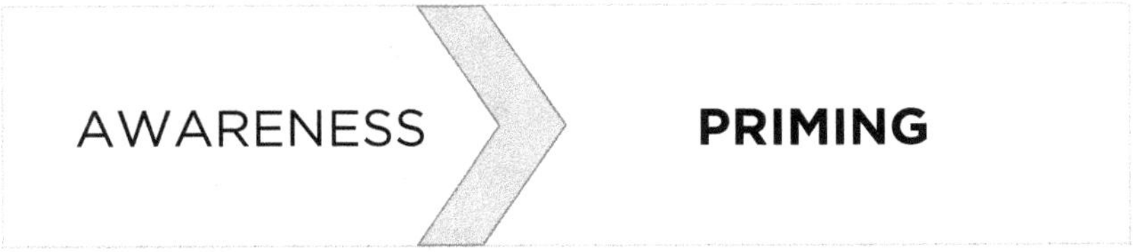

Virtually every traditional book about brand building begins with the need to create *brand awareness,* the necessary foundation upon which the whole brand structure is built. Brand awareness refers to people's ability to identify a given brand, and the probability that a certain brand name will come into the mind of a potential customer. I agree; brand awareness is an absolute *sine qua non* in consumer decision-making. If a brand name is not recalled in the context of seeking a product or service, the brand will not be considered when the buying choice is made. But brand awareness is simply an intellectual exercise. As such, it is insufficient to building real, sustainable relationships with the brand, and insufficient to building an emotional, lasting connection. Therefore, it is insufficient to building a BRAND*cebo.*

As savvy marketers develop and communicate the foundational elements of their brand, they should remember that BRAND*cebo* effects are *not* the province of conscious, rational, linear, logical thought; the objective part of the mind must be respected and courted, too. We do that when we offer information and reasoned arguments. But to evoke the real BRAND*cebo* magic, you have to step into the messy, emotional, subconscious mind—the part that makes decisions based upon intangibles other than fact and reasoning.

We've seen already that it's quite possible for brands to engage with human emotions and, therefore, the body, completely bypassing the logical mind. Paul Zak, an economist and neurobiologist and the founding Director of the Center for Neuroeconomic Studies at Claremont Graduate University, has found that oxytocin, the neurochemical that mediates love and attachment (the same molecule that's triggered when you're held or touched by a loved one) is released in people's brains when they're asked about brands they love[18]. Scientists from Duke University have shown that emotion and value are handled by the same part of the brain—the ventromedial prefrontal cortex, which is responsible for determining risk and fear—weakening our ability to make impartial judgments about economic value over desire[19].

These emotional and neurochemical factors exist in moment-by-moment purchasing decisions as well as in long-term brand relationships. A 2013 survey across seven different B2B industries found that personal value (based on emotion) had twice as much influence as business value (based on logic/reason)[20].

The power of emotions in consumer decision-making is cross-cultural; it is not limited to developed western nations. East or West, consumers need to be emotionally engaged in order to fall in love with a brand. In China (where annual consumer spending is expected to soar from $2.03 trillion in 2010 to $6.5 trillion in 2020[21]), a major 2013 study found that emotional factors ranked first as a reason to buy for more than half of the categories examined[22].

To engage with consumers on an emotional level, marketers must delve into their customers' desires and yearnings while crafting messages that build brand awareness. Remember that these deeply stored desires may be very different from rational needs, but this is where the power is. And it's this power into which the BRAND*cebo* taps.

To begin with, think about your product or service in light of consumers' deep longings: What do they crave? To what do they aspire? As you tell your story to potential consumers, shine the light on the transformative experience your product will provide that is related to their deep longings. Sculpt your brand and product messages to elicit passionate aspiration, not just utility. You may also choose to offer some information about practical features on what you are selling; these will satisfy the conscious, rational overseer in the mind, but the real emotional juice comes from plugging your product into the core yearnings of the hidden self. Emotion is a direct connection to the underbelly of the mind.

Consider thinking of a brand as a person, with its own story, personality, and idiosyncrasies, rather than as a robot-like mechanical collection of parts. Robots don't communicate through symbols, stories, subtexts, and non-verbal cues, but an effective brand does.

Like poetry, effective brands build in creative elements, like images, symbols, sensory effects, and so forth, that encompass deep longings, aspirations, and emotions. The result is a connection to the rich, unconscious processes of the human mind. This, in turn, makes the BRAND*cebo* effect possible.

While Nike shoes and the ringing of bells are examples of unconditioned stimuli used by researchers to study this kind of Priming, other kinds of unconditioned stimuli are more useful to poets of marketing.

Visual images, for example, are hugely powerful. Certain kinds of pictures produce states of emotional arousal. Pictures of sexy bodies pique sexual readiness, pictures of food throw the digestive system into a fever of preparation, while pictures of babies or of anything that shares what Konrad Lorenz called "the baby schema[23]" (large eyes, small nose, retreating chin, and bulging forehead), trigger physiological caretaking behavior. When a marketing campaign repeatedly pairs a brand with these types of visual images, Priming occurs. Eventually, the brand itself triggers the body physiologically.

Take, for example, the following ad[24]:

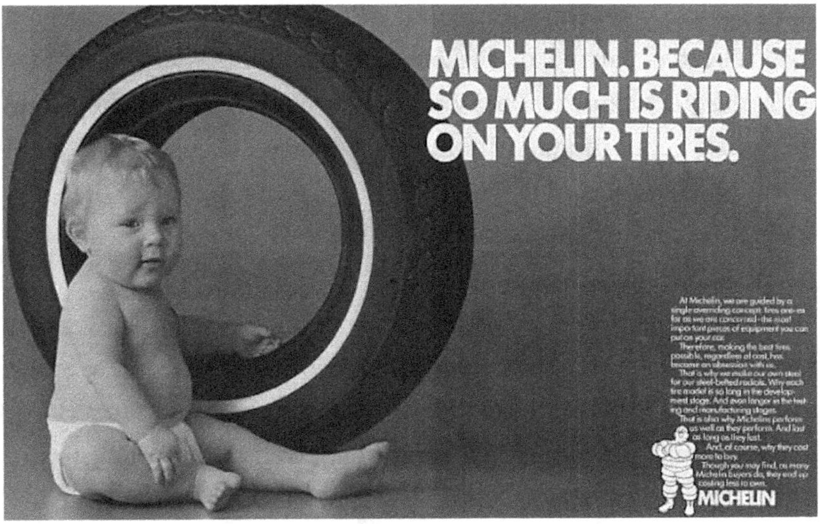

This memorable and powerful ad does *not* focus on information about the material, design, or testing of Michelin's tires. In fact, the wordy part of the message occupies remarkably small acreage in the spread. Instead, this ad goes for the ultimate emotional driver—a photo of a baby, the sort of picture that has been demonstrated (using fMRI) to increase activation of the brain's nucleus accumbens, the area central to motivation and reward.

Nucleus accumbens (circled)[25]

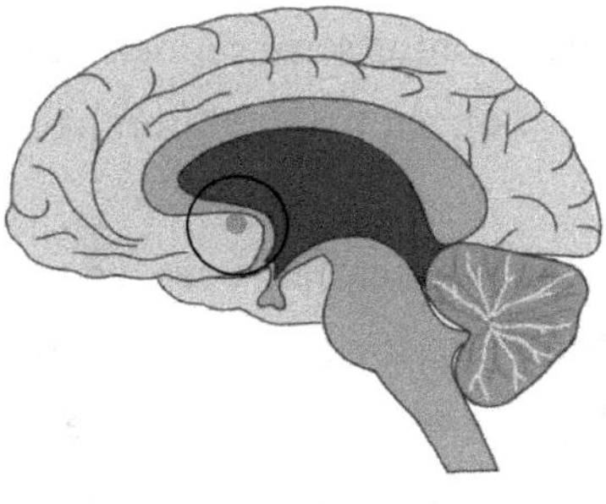

Knowing what we know about Priming, we can understand that repeated pairing of the brand name and "Michelin" image with the picture of the baby will eventually result in the brand becoming a conditioned stimulus that alone will trigger the arousal of the nucleus accumbens and the caretaking behavior that will lead to purchasing the safest tires possible. "I care about my baby's safety" = "I buy Michelin."

This same type of Priming can come into play whenever any image that causes a physiological response is part of a brand message. Scantily clad beauties ornamenting boats or cars? Hard-bodied hunks promoting perfumes or jewelry? Mouth-watering images of juicy cheeseburgers? Even the Disney's brand-carrier, Mickey Mouse, has evolved since the 1920s to more closely fit the cute baby schema—with head and eyes grown bigger while the nose retreats closer to the face—in order to trigger caretaking behavior[26].

None of this has to do with logic; all of it has to do with the appeal to the unconscious underside of the human mind—the area where BRAND*cebo* effects can occur.

THE COFFEE WE CRAVE

Almost 80% of American adults are regular coffee drinkers[27]. This means approximately a quarter of a billion people in the US drink coffee each day.

The addictive qualities of caffeine are legendary; just be around a "coffee person" who's late for his or her morning cup of joe. It's not a pretty sight. Regular coffee drinkers are not just Conditioned by the caffeine they consume but also by the time of day it's consumed, the coffee shop signage and logo, and even the sounds associated with the experience[28]. If you're a coffee drinker, you know the feeling: just the sight of your favorite coffee shop stimulates you as you anticipate your preferred brew. In other words, you have a physical, conditioned response and you haven't even had your caffeine.

Coffee drinkers exposed to the logo, packaging, and attributes of their favorite coffee brand result in a heightened experience—and get this—they experience the same emotions even when the coffee they consume is a different brand than their favorite one. Sounds a bit like the Coke/Pepsi experience, doesn't it? And it helps explain the staggering success of coffee chains like Starbucks.

Breaking this down in terms of Priming and the placebo effect, caffeine plays the role of the unconditioned response: you are wired to be affected by caffeine; it's not something you learn to feel. The conditioned stimuli, then, are time of day, signage, logo, and the associated sounds of coffee making (you can just hear the hissing of the espresso machine, can't you?). Once this association is repeated often enough, the Conditioned *response* is an elated experience before the caffeine is even consumed.

THE COLOR OF PRIMING

Similarly, color comes freighted with its own subliminal power as we nurture brand awareness. Since the early 1900s, there has been substantial research investigating of the emotional messages of colors.

Some messages may be culturally learned, but some of them appear to be inborn, judging from the fact that they are consistent across cultures. Many of the world's most powerful brands are known by their colors: Jet Blue airline; IBM's nickname, Big Blue; McDonald's Golden Arches; the United States' Red, White, and Blue, and its Red State/Blue State political parties; UPS' slogan, "What can Brown do for you?"; and The Cincinnati Reds baseball team are just a few examples. These brands and many others intentionally engage colors to reach out subliminally to their audiences. Canny brand planners will never ignore color, and what the colors they choose say about their business.

It's beyond the scope of this book to discuss color psychology in detail—much is already available elsewhere—but the ability of color to connect with unconscious processes in the brain is so great that no BRAND*cebo*-aware marketer should ignore it. So, let's look at one example: the power of red.

In 2005, two British anthropologists analyzed the results of the 2004 Summer Olympic matches in boxing, *tae kwon do,* and wrestling, in which competitors were randomly assigned red or blue clothing[29]. They found that when the opponents were otherwise well matched, the one wearing red was significantly more likely to win. (The red effect applied when fighters were properly matched with an opponent, not when they were seriously overmatched in their bouts.)

Three years later, the same researchers broadened the scope of their investigation to include the teams of England's soccer Premier League from 1947 to 2003[30]. Their analysis showed that football teams wearing red jerseys had a significantly higher likelihood of both winning home games and winning the title than teams wearing either yellow or orange jerseys.

The findings were unequivocal: three out of the four most successful English clubs donned red jerseys for home games—

Manchester United's "Devils," Liverpool F.C. "Reds," and Arsenal F.C.

Knowing this background about the power of red, think about the color decision that went into department store Target's logo selection. Or look closely at the almost monochromatic Tesla logo and observe how it is carefully punctuated with deep, stimulating red.

But images are not the only creative elements that can serve as unconditioned stimuli as we build brand awareness. Music can subliminally contain physiological rhythms (such as heart rate, breathing, and brain waves) to match the rate of its rhythmic pulses. Marketers who want to pair their brand with a high-energy experience may choose music with quick rhythms, which will tend to speed up the heart rate and make listeners feel jazzed and upbeat. If "mellow" is the effect they are going for, they may choose rhythms that are slower than the 60-80 beats per minute of an adult resting heart rate.

THE POWER OF PRIMING

With Pavlov's dog experiments dating back to the dawn of the 20th century, Priming may be the best-understood way in which to engage with the unconscious mind.

In his acclaimed book, *Thinking, Fast and Slow,* Nobel Prize-winning psychologist Daniel Kahneman, reported on a study in which groups of students were given questionnaires about how happy they were[31]. All surveys included two questions, but some posed one question first and some posed the other first.

The questions were:

1. On a scale of 1 to 5, how happy are you these days (5 being the happiest)?
2. How many dates did you have last month or dinner parties did you attend?

When the happiness question came first, there was no correlation between the students' response to the two questions, but when the question about their social life came first, the correlation between the two items was very strong: students who had had more dates or attended more parties rated their happiness much higher. This shows how strong context is in eliciting response.

By Priming your audience beforehand with cues to understand your message in a certain way, you can, to a great extent, control their response and the mindset in which you want them to be thinking about your brand. Companies link inspirational celebrities, objects, environments, or aspirational messages with their brands to Prime consumers' responses in the same way that the question about dates and parties Primed the students' evaluations of their own happiness.

9 OUT OF 10

At my own branding company, Ameba Marketing, I had a client who participated in an industry-wide annual customer satisfaction survey conducted by a state's institute for quality. The format for these surveys involved giving the participant a series of statements about the quality of service they received, and asking them to rate it on a scale of one to ten with one being "Strongly Disagree," and 10 being "Strongly Agree."

For example, a customer might be presented with the statement: "My calls get answered in less than one minute," or "The person I spoke with was knowledgeable and helpful," or "The information I received solved my problem or need."

The higher the overall score the company received, the more it was rewarded with stars, credentials, and industry prestige. The key, though, was to get a high percentage of either nine or ten scores, in order to qualify for the institute's "highest" ranking.

As we studied the campaign brief and prepared our strategy, we reviewed pertinent performance data provided by the client. Interestingly, the data showed that about 90% of the client's customer-service calls are answered in less than one minute; that 90% of these calls result in a satisfactory solution, and; over 90% of the customers are very happy or extremely happy with the client's service (as determined by an independent survey conducted by the client).

Armed with this great data, we ran a multi-faceted "nine-out-of-ten" campaign that included an internet and social media campaign, radio ads, and direct mail. We never mentioned the survey; instead we presented our target with messages like, "Nine out of ten customers say they're extremely satisfied with our service," or "Nine out of ten customer service calls are answered in less than one minute." We simply shared real and truthful company data, and along the way, associated the brand with the numbers "nine" and "ten." During the next customer satisfaction survey, responses of nine and ten rose by an incredible 21%, which garnered the client the coveted "high" ranking. This is the power of Priming.

PRIMETIME MUSIC

Music, as a type of Prime, can affect purchasing. In one experiment, researchers played, on alternating days at a grocery store wine display, music that was recognizably French or German[32]. After two weeks, the amount of each nation's wine purchases were tallied. The results were definitive: more French wine was sold on days when French music played, and more German wine was sold on the German music days. A simple, auditory Prime—background music—demonstrably influenced buying behavior in ways that consumers were not consciously aware.

Musical Priming can also affect how customers experience a product. In another experiment[33], researchers chose four pieces of background music with four distinctive qualities: "*Carmina Burana*" by Carl Orff was powerful and heavy, *Waltz of the Flowers* from Tchaikovsky's *Nutcracker Suite* was subtle and refined, *Just Can't Get Enough* by Nouvelle Vague was zingy and refreshing, and *Slow Breakdown* by Michael Brook was mellow and soft.

Subsequently, participants were given wine—the same wine—while each of the four musical selections played in the background. They were then asked to describe the taste of the wine. When the researchers compared the taste descriptions with the background music, they found that people described the wine's tastes in accordance with the type of music they heard. The ones who heard *Carmina Burana* were more likely to describe the wine as "powerful and heavy," while the ones who listened to *Waltz of the Flowers* were more likely to describe it as "subtle and refined," and so forth, proof that subtle, even subliminal, Priming can make all the difference in how a product is perceived.

Here's another example of the power of the Prime: In a creativity test participants who were Primed with the Apple brand (associated with innovation and creativity; "Think Different") significantly outperformed participants who were Primed with the IBM brand (associated with tradition; smart and responsible)[34]. Similarly, participants in that study who were Primed with the Disney Channel logo (associated with honesty and sincerity) behaved more honestly in a test than participants who were exposed to the E-Channel logo (apparently not associated with honesty and sincerity)[35]. These are both strong indicators that powerful brands, themselves, can act as behavioral Primes.

THE FAMILIARITY HEURISTIC

A subset of Priming involves using familiarity to predispose people to choose in a certain direction. Have you ever wondered about the purpose of those political posters and signs that simply state the candidate's name? There is no information, no issues, no argument—just the name. Those signs are taking advantage of the Familiarity Heuristic, the well-documented tendency of humans to overestimate the value of the familiar and judge it more desirable than the novel[36].

In one Stanford study published in 2011, Ab Litt and his team found that participants tended to choose the task (in this case a puzzle) that they were told was created by someone with whom they had some passing familiarity, even when they knew that the puzzle would be longer and more difficult[37]. This preference for the familiar was strongest when the participants were put under time pressure to complete the puzzle within a limited time.

This research suggests that when you are building brand Priming, just the act of putting your logo, name, or product image in front of people—in other words, making it *familiar*—

strongly enhances their likelihood of choosing it when the time comes to shop.

A BRAND-PRIMING TRIFECTA

Taken together, Priming and the Familiarity Heuristic are potent channels for communicating with the unconscious thought processes that are the territory in which BRAND*cebo* effects occur. When they work together effectively and synergistically, they can harness the power and creativity of the subconscious mind and put it at your service.

You may have noticed, for instance, that when you flip through a magazine and see an ad for a mega brand like Cartier, Chanel, Rolex, or Armani, it is often not accompanied by any words. The ad may simply consist of a beautiful image and the brand's logo. That's it; that's all that's needed; no clever headline or catchy slogan.

These brands have done their work well through Priming and familiarity, and the messages have been conveyed simply, yet effectively. *You* play the copywriter role. And so is every single person looking at the ads. It takes only a second for you to look at that wordless picture and the creative, emotional part of your brain immediately offers you the most compelling thoughts, imaginings, desires, aspirations, and cravings best aligned with your deepest longings in ways that no copywriter could ever create. If a million people looked at that ad, there would be a million variations of those emotions, each unique to the viewer.

WHAT WE BELIEVE WE BECOME

When we view the placebo effect through the lens of Priming, we see the first element of the placebo equation: what a customer believes, or what he or she are led to believe. We have scientific evidence proving the mind/body connection isn't just woo-woo voodoo, but real enough to affect us mentally, emotionally, and physically. And we can see that effective branding actually imprints itself deep within our brains to affect our tastes and buying preferences.

This effect is so powerful that it raises certain questions for us as we build our brand awareness: how can we engage with Priming and familiarity in an ethical way, especially among vulnerable younger consumers, in order to shape purchasing decisions? What is the optimal balance between argumentation and information appealing to the rational mind and emotional cues appealing to the impulsive, emotional, non-rational mind?

HOW TO BRAND*cebo* PRIMING?

1. Cater to passions, not needs.
2. Capture hearts; the brain will follow.
3. They deserve an expert; be one.
4. First earn their trust, then promise.
5. Be familiar with and connect to their aspirations.

Brand building is collaboration between the purveyor, i.e., the company and its brand, and the consumer. The process creates an exchange of information, trust building, and finally a relationship that creates an Expectation of success.

In the next chapter, I explore the second element in the BRAND*cebo* equation—Expectation—and how it transforms consumers from bystanders with merely a positive *perception* of a brand to true believers who *expect* to self-actualize through it.

Chapter 5

Expectation: Branding & the Art of the Self-fulfilling Prophecy

How to Turn Brand Perception into Performance Expectation

We all, hopefully, subscribe to the Golden Rule: do unto others as you would have them do unto you. We genuinely strive to treat everyone equally, regardless of their race, income, gender, or any other demographic or ethnic characteristic. This is our conscious thought controlling much of how we behave.

At least that's what we'd like to believe. Research, however, shows subconscious discrepancies between what we think we believe and what we ultimately do. While that's a subject for another book, or many of them, what's interesting for this book is the unexpected and often unrecognized biases that are common even among the most equality-oriented zealots among us.

Consider the following, for example: we treat tall people differently and more positively than we treat short people.

Malcolm Gladwell, the bestselling author of *Blink: The Power of*

Thinking without Thinking, surveyed half of America's Fortune 500 companies, and among many other questions asked about the height of their CEOs[1]. His findings were astounding.

While the average American male is 5'9", the average CEO was almost six feet tall. It gets more interesting. Only 14.5% of American men are six feet or taller, yet a full 58% of the CEOs fell within this range. On average, only 3.9% of US men are 6'2" or taller, yet even there the CEOs had vastly outnumbered the general population with 30% of CEOs reaching these heights.

Clearly, we like tall CEOs. But is height really a factor in leadership, intelligence, and the complex social skills necessary to lead a Fortune 500 company?

It also pays to be tall. Timothy Judge and Daniel Cable studied the effect of height on the amount of money earned[2]. They found that for every inch above average the person's height, they earned an average of $789 more per year. This applied to men and women, alike. In Judge's words, "The process of literally 'looking down on others' may cause one to be more confident. Similarly, having others 'looking up to us' may instill in tall people more self-confidence[3]."

We could assume that, at a subconscious level, when we "look up" to someone, as we did in childhood with our parents and teachers, we expect them to be more knowledgeable and have more authority. This Expectation then affects our behavior towards them, even if we don't realize it. Expectation is the second element in the placebo equation and a critical component in our everyday beliefs and actions.

EXPECTATION DEFINED

Before we dig deeper into Expectation and its role in the world of the placebo effect, let's first define what it is we're talking about.

The Merriam-Webster Dictionary gives us this basic definition of Expectation: "a belief that something will happen or is likely to happen[4]."

One set of researchers defines Expectation as an individual's prediction of likely outcomes based on current events[5]. Others expand it into the context of the placebo effect in medicine. Expectation in this case meaning an individual's belief in a treatment, such as a pill, that results in actual healing occurring even though the treatment contained no medicinal properties. One could think of placebos as techniques used to manipulate an individual's Expectation. These are all variations on the same theme.

Earlier we saw Priming in the context of "as we believe, so we are." With Expectation it's "as we expect, so we are." Regardless of the nuances of definition, the mind-body link continues to strengthen.

THE HEALING POWERS OF EXPECTATION

Throughout Mexico, and extending down through the countries of Central and South America, traditional healers have played a ubiquitous and vital role. Where, for centuries, the availability of "modern" medicine was limited-to-nonexistent, these healers have served as physicians, psychologists, and priests all rolled into one. The crazy thing is they were effective.

In Mexico, *curanderos* (practitioners of folk medicine; female: *curanderas*) perform the role of traditional healers. Although more common in the past, the tradition is alive and well today. Much of Mexico still consists of rural villages, with local people living close to the land. These healers have been part of life here for centuries, and trust in their skills and healing powers is deeply engrained within the culture. Whether the afflicted are physically or mentally ill, in geographic areas without doctors or formal medical systems, they go to their local healer. This isn't unusual, risky, or New Age "woo-woo" as it would be in our culture. Instead, it's absolutely normal.

The *curandero* doesn't don a headdress and feathers above a paint-slathered face, as we have seen in movies. In fact, he would probably look completely normal and is likely to have been trained in traditional healing arts, or have a natural ability in healing, or both.

The healing itself consists of *pláticas*—talks, prayers, and rituals. It might include smudging (the burning of herbs), repeating prayers, drinking water at a certain time of day for a certain duration of time, or even burying a special stick in a field or road—things we might consider useless. However, the Mexican villagers' strong belief and Expectation in the healing powers of the *curandero* does the work for them.

Researchers Robert Trotter and Juan Antonio Chavira said, "The religious and spiritual aspects of the healing process capitalize on the patients' faith and belief systems. The use of herbs, fruits, eggs, and oils allows healing to occur through the use of everyday resources, products the patient can easily obtain[6]."

The astounding thing about *curandismo* is its effectiveness. The patient believes in the healing and expects it to happen, and therefore it does. It might not work in Stage 4 cancer, but with a plethora of illnesses, from every day ailments to chronic diseases, it is successful.

How does this happen? Are the smudged herbs deeply medicinal? Does the burying of a stick use a secret illness-relieving muscle? Do the prayers trigger a physiological healing process?

The answer is shockingly simple. Patients expect to be healed. This Expectation is powerful enough to affect their body physiologically, measurably, and with enough power to cure them.

But these are tales, you might say. Exaggerated stories from the wilderness, told by bearded, feverish travelers. Or fairy tales, like the King's Touch in Chapter 2. Well, buckle up, because they are more than tall tales...

THE PRICE OF PAIN

In 2008, an extensive research project was conducted on the relationship between the price of a good and its expected effectiveness[7]. Do people expect a product to be better only because it costs more? Conversely, do they assume a cheaper product will underperform? If they do believe in it, does this sheer Expectation have any real, measurable effect?

The researchers began by studying pain. They wanted to understand the effects of placebo painkillers and their corresponding price. Would a higher-priced painkiller be more effective in its treatment of pain than a lower-priced one despite the fact that both were placebos and theoretically ineffective?

Eighty-two pain-free volunteers were first presented with a brochure explaining the wonders of a new painkilling drug, much like codeine but with a faster response time. Half the participants were told that each pill cost $2.50 while the other half were told it cost 10 cents each—a significant difference. Each pill was actually a placebo and should have had the same effect as a glass of water.

Both before and after the placebo painkiller was taken, electrical shocks were applied to participants' wrists. Participants were then interviewed on their pain reduction or lack thereof. Would either pill work at all? Would price be a factor?

Results showed that 61% of individuals taking the cheaper placebo experienced pain reduction, so right off we knew the placebo effect was working. But the kicker was that 85% of those taking the "expensive" placebo experienced less pain; 39% more individuals experienced pain relief from the more expensive painkiller than from the less costly pill.

Both placebos were shown to work, however price was a significant factor in their corresponding efficacy, clearly demonstrating that we expect more expensive products to work better. Participants had expected both "painkillers" to work, and they expected the expensive one to be more effective; they were right on both counts.

Researchers` conclusions weren't just that price was a factor in making the power of Expectation stronger. They went further to point out the positive physical potential of great marketing. "Promoting the efficacy of a medication can have significant improvements to a consumer's health. Advertising, if done well, can give rise to a positive placebo effect[8]."

PASTA ALWAYS TASTES BETTER IN ITALY

The power of Expectation doesn't just work in remote Mexican and Central American villages, or in the controlled and pristine environment of a scientific study. Expectation drives each of us, all day, every day.

Almost every day you can see, either in a shop or online, a sign advertising a sale. We see the sign and we expect to find a bargain. Part of our reaction is Priming. In that a conditioned stimulus, "sale," creates a conditioned response, we shop whether we need whatever is on sale or not. But we can add to this the Expectation that we're getting a bargain price. After all, why else would it be on sale? So we go in and buy it, expecting, correctly or incorrectly, that we got a great deal.

If you've been to Italy, you might have noticed how much better the pasta tastes there. You may have ordered the same Carbonara that you order at your local and very authentic Italian restaurant, but sitting in that café in Italy, surrounded by the language and the streets and the smells, it just tastes better.

How about a dram of scotch in Scotland? You're in a pub on a dark and stormy evening and you order a brand you've never heard of before. That evening, it's the best scotch you've ever tasted. You buy a bottle, take it home, and upon your next sip discover that it's just average after all. The scenario would be the same whether it's sushi in Japan, a steak in Texas, or a bagel and lox in New York City.

We expect the local food and drink to taste better in their home environs. In some cases, it might actually be better, but in other cases, it's simply the power of Expectation that made that average scotch taste like manna from heaven in the appropriate setting.

Mama Aida, my grandmother and a mega brand in and of herself, makes the best meatballs in the universe. Sitting down to eat a bowl of her meatballs, I'm taken back to the comfort of home and the Expectation that these will be the very best meatballs because they always were when I was a kid.

My mother is the best cook I know. She has my grandmother's meatball recipe, and makes it exactly the same way. Those meatballs are excellent, yet somehow not quite as good. The setting, the atmosphere, the smells, the sounds, the memories, and my grandmother's smile all combined to create powerful Priming and Expectation that, together, embodied a secret, unduplicatable ingredient that made those meatballs so irresistible.

THE MECHANICS OF EXPECTATION

As with so much in life, we don't actually know how Expectation works within the placebo effect. There's no physical element we can place on a slide and view under a microscope; there are no moving parts or widgets we can reverse engineer and recreate. Researchers haven't yet been able to clearly map the cognitive process by which Expectation creates measurable physiological outcomes.

One view suggests that positive expectations help individuals reduce stress and anxiety. As there is a direct correlation between reducing these two factors and improving the strength of the immune system, logic dictates that the stronger body will perform better[9].

In cases of severe chronic pain, research has shown positive expectations may very well be the trigger that allows people to conduct something resembling a normal life[10]. Positive expectations allowed these individuals to change their worldviews. Within the constant fog of pain, they were able focus on hope, distracting them from their painful illness. With an improved attitude and spirit came a corresponding reduction in pain[11].

But the above theories are based on unhealthy individuals with positive expectations. They do not explain either the quick response by healthy individuals to painkiller placebos or the deadly effect of a negative Expectation, as in Chapter 2's witchdoctor-induced voodoo deaths.

This gap is perhaps best addressed by the Response Expectancy Theory[12]. This theory states that Expectation is an actual emotional response, much like relief from the reduction of pain. The mere anticipation of this response triggers physiological changes, such as increased blood pressure, heart rate, and skin conductance. These bodily changes happen immediately, without lag.

For example, you might feel the painful sting of the needle just by looking at the approaching syringe. Or you might get goosebumps just by imagining the ice-cold temperature of the pool water you're about to jump into.

Even though we don't understand exactly how Expectation works within the placebo effect, we do know many things about the results. Once again, we look to fMRI for a deeper understanding of the whys behind the physiological changes. Images help us connect observable behavior with corresponding, real-time brain activity.

As with the previous example, researchers set out to study pain in volunteers. However, this time participants were slid into an fMRI scanner for the tests[13]. Using warm-to-painfully-hot stimuli, researchers monitored participants' brain activity.

In this study, critical to understanding the effect of Expectation, before participants actually received the promised pain, researchers told them what type of pain to expect and how severe it would be. Imagine your response if you were just told you were about to be jabbed by something sharp and hot, and it would hurt like the dickens. My brain activity fired up just from writing the words. Yours has too, by the way.

Needless to say, those subjects who anticipated pain had extremely heightened brain activity. Specifically, the anterior cingulate cortex and the anterior insula lit up. The former is involved in autonomic functions, like heart rate and blood pressure, along with higher, emotional responses such as impulse control and reward anticipation[14]. The latter is involved in self-awareness and various levels of cognitive functioning[15].

The activity in these areas during the pain study increased before any actual stimulus was applied. Just by messing with someone's Expectation, a real physiological brain response occurred with that anticipated stimulus.

In a 2004 article in Science, researchers again worked with pain and fMRI[16]. This time, they examined the effect of placebo painkillers and what specific activity they elicited within the brain. They stated, "In two functional magnetic resonance imaging (fMRI) experiments, we found that placebo analgesia was related to decreased brain activity in pain-sensitive brain regions, including the thalamus, insula, and anterior cingulate cortex, and was associated with increased activity during anticipation of pain in the prefrontal cortex, providing evidence that placebos alter the experience of pain."

In short, whether given a placebo or not, the mere Expectation of an increase or decrease in pain is enough to get the brain to light up and respond.

EXPENSIVE WINE TASTES BETTER

Fortunately, this same fMRI technology can be used for more pleasant research venues, such as wine tasting. This time, researchers added price into the equation, much as they did with the expensive vs. cheap painkiller pill study. Researcher asked whether the Expectation of an expensive versus cheaper wine would affect brain activity.

Willing participants were presented with two wine glasses, each with a sampling of wine[17]. They were told that one wine costs $90 a bottle while the other only $10, when in fact the exact same wine was in both glasses. Logically, participants would expect the expensive stuff to taste better. True to form, the fMRIs showed significantly greater activity in the pleasure center of the brain, the orbitofrontal cortex, when participants sipped what they thought was the expensive wine.

The Orbitofrontal Cortex[18]

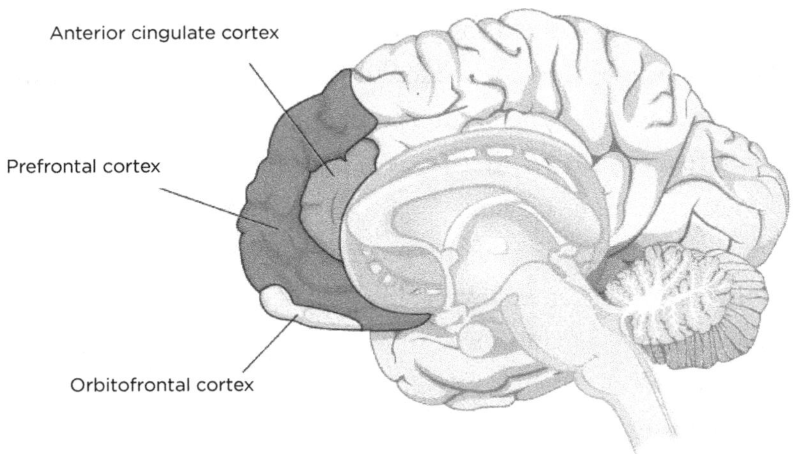

When sipping from the other glass and expecting an inferior experience, there was a decrease in activity in the exact same area of participants' brains, the pleasure center. Participants experienced greater pleasure when they thought they were drinking better wine. This Expectancy actually modified their brain chemistry.

Powerful stuff, indeed.

THINK HEALTHY, AND YOU'LL LIVE LONGER

Just how far can the Expectation of the placebo effect go? If it can reduce pain and make cheap wine more fun; can it make us healthier, too?

A 2007 study worked to answer just this question[19]. Researchers gathered 84 participants, all women and all housekeepers in seven different hotels.

First, researchers gathered a baseline assessment of individuals' health. They measured weight, blood pressure, waist size, etc., and then they separated them into two groups. The first group was told that their job, alone, provided them with enough exercise on a daily basis to meet the amount recommended by the Surgeon General for a healthy, fit lifestyle. They were given Priming information to back this up.

The second group? You guessed it. They didn't receive any of the above information and were, in effect, a control group.

Each group was monitored to make sure participants' normal behavior didn't change. No one got it into their head to train for a triathlon, for example. Rather, they kept up with their daily lives.

At the end of four weeks, all participants' health was measured again. The control group's health, not surprisingly, didn't change, however, women in the group that believed that they performed the recommended amount of activity had lost weight, experienced a significant reduction in body fat, and reduced their waist sizes, all in comparison to the control group. The placebo element of Expectation served to make these housekeepers healthier though they did nothing else to improve their health.

In a similar study, researchers found that elderly individuals who simply perceived their health to be better, regardless of whether it was true, actually lived longer[20]. As you think, so you live. Those elderly individuals who thought they were in poor health? They were six times more likely to die than their positive-thinking counterparts[21].

Something astounding is happening in our midst.

THE POWER OF EXPECTATION

For a skeptic, each of the above examples could be considered an isolated, theoretical study far removed from everyday life. The excitement over an expensive glass of wine or the fear of being jabbed with a needle in a research lab has no real impact on the overwhelming efficacy of drugs and chemicals, right? Wrong.

Consider the following study involving pregnant women with morning sickness[22]. These volunteers were actually pregnant and actually experienced morning sickness. The nauseated women were told they were being given an anti-emetic (anti-nausea) drug. They took the drug, and not only felt less nauseous but also, physiologically, had a significantly reduced amount of nausea-induced stomach movement. But true to the bizarre minds of research scientists, the women were actually given the opposite of an anti-nausea drug—they were given a nausea-*inducing* drug. These innocent, soon-to-be-child-bearing women should have felt absolutely horrible during the trial. However, they expected the drug they were given to reduce their nausea and it did—in mind and body.

Harking back to brands as relationships, the power of Expectation can be found in Fournier's seven types of relationships, too. Personal commitment, in which partners are committed to each other through good times and bad, shows an Expectation that each party will remain committed.

Interestingly, intimacy is also a relationship type that improves with Expectation. Once a deep level of understanding has been reached, the Expectation is that it will be honored and continued. So, while brands are relationships, these relationships are often steeped in the power of the three elements of the placebo.

As a child playing soccer in the neighborhoods of Jerusalem, being told that I "played like Cruyff" meant not only that I believed in it, but I also expected it to be accurate. The next logical step after belief was the Expectation that I really would play like Cruyff. In high school, when my new coach switched me to a sweeper, I no longer expected to play like Cruyff, because I wasn't in his position. However, I could easily expect to play like Beckenbauer when I was told by my coach that my playing style resembled his.

What was crucial for my belief and Expectation was the fact that I loved the "brands" Cruyf and Beckenbauer, and trusted both sources of praise. It turns out that trust is a key component of effective Expectation. If the Mexican villagers hadn't been inculcated by a culture steeped in the belief in traditional healers, they wouldn't have expected much from them. This crack in the foundation of belief would weaken the overall effect.

When it comes to pregnant women experiencing morning sickness, what if an unknown person in flip-flops and wearing a T-shirt had offered them an amazing pill that would stop them from feeling sick? Compare this to being told by a clean-cut, professional-looking doctor in a white cloak that the pill was the safest, newest, and most effective drug around.

The powerful phenomenon of Expectation appears in many aspects of our lives. Let's say you have a friend who tries every new weight-loss diet that comes around, yet despite all his effort, he is still 30 pounds overweight and pre-diabetic. To support him, you try the latest fad, too. You don't lose an ounce. But then your fitness instructor at the gym tells you of a scientific discovery written up in the *Journal of Nutrition* about the very same diet. This time when you try it, you lose those extra ten pounds and feel like you're 20-years-old again. Voila!

If you're exposed to information from a credible source about the efficacy of the placebo, you operate from a position of confidence and expect the drug to work. The placebo is well set to function.

While Priming was mostly subconscious, Expectation can work from both the conscious and subconscious levels. The first two elements of Expectation—receiving credible information and choosing to believe in that information—are both conscious.

For example, having the diet recommended by the fitness instructor and following that diet are both conscious elements. However, having the diet actually work for you while it doesn't work for your overweight friend demonstrates the subconscious level of Expectation. Both you and your friend had no control over the outcome. Conscious expectations can work together with subconscious Priming.

WHAT TINY LOVE CAN DO TO CHILD DEVELOPMENT

I've been working for over 15 years with Tiny Love, one of the world's most notable developmental toy companies. Since its inception, the company cleverly positioned itself not just as toy manufacturers but also as providers of a stimulating system for child development. They had conducted years of research with child psychologists to develop their toys, which they firmly believed would stimulate child development.

We built a marketing program around the idea of a child development system. Utilizing scientific data from the company's research, we were easily able to instill the belief that our toys were better because they stimulated certain aspects of babies' natural development (all very true, by the way). Because of this belief, parents expected their child to be more developed physically and cognitively than other babies. Their motivation for their children to be the best and brightest was a given. In fact, the marketing concept worked so well that this toy manufacturer was able to effectively compete in the children's toy market with products that were significantly more expensive than similar toys in their category.

Following in the wake of Tiny Love, a different company developed a series of DVDs called Baby Einstein. Just by its choice of name, this company suggested that if children listened to these DVDs they would become smarter and better developed than their peers. Parents expected these DVDs to truly make their children smarter.

While no formal studies that I know of were conducted to verify whether this worked or not, the anecdotal evidence is astounding[23]. This is what one mother had to say: "My son was a very late talker. We were trying everything. My husband brought home Baby Shakespeare one day and (thank goodness) he just started talking from that moment on. Now every time a new video comes out we are there[24]."

And another: "My twenty-month-old son has adored Baby Mozart, Baby Bach, Baby Newton, and Baby Van Gogh for five months now. He is talking in sentences, and has been for two months now. He is also learning his colors thanks to Baby Van Gogh! We could not think of better 'shows' to fill his little mind with at this age[25]."

BUILDING BRAND*cebo*
Step 2: From Perception to Expectation

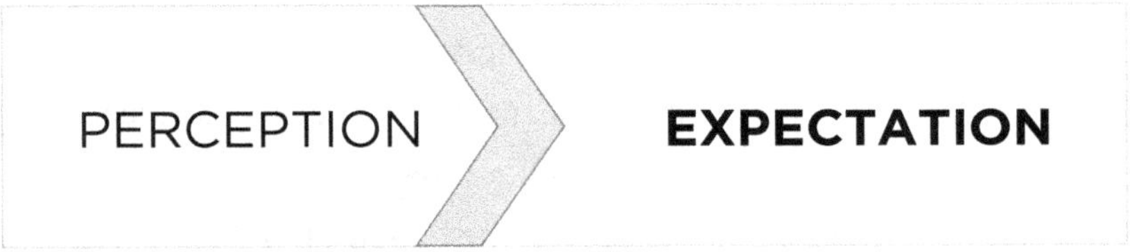

Brand Perception, like brand awareness, is something that exists in the minds of consumers. It is the sum of all associations that consumers apply to a brand. It goes far beyond the simple awareness that a brand exists. If awareness-building strategies are successful, a positive perception is created and it is likely that interest in the brand will rise dramatically.

Yet just like brand awareness, perception is a matter of the mind with little to no cognitively tangible values. Positive brand perception may result in a great affinity for the brand and its products but lacks the elements of real anticipation to experience the promised, and believed (remember Priming?) outcomes. The genuine Expectation is that the brand will deliver superior performance.

HAVE YOU DRIVEN A TESLA LATELY?

Consider the expectations raised by the Tesla brand. Tesla makes a great car that will take you safely from point A to point B and helps the environment in the process. Now that's great, but it would be hard to justify the Tesla's price tag—close to $100,000—for these normal expectations. A Toyota Prius is perceived as delivering pretty much the same for one-third of the cost.

But somehow, in addition to technological bells and whistles, Tesla marketers have created a beautiful story with you, the hero, in the driver's seat. They've built the anticipation that driving a Tesla will be a very special experience. They've created a performance Expectation that makes that hefty price tag seem reasonable—a bargain at any price. Just look at their interactive print campaign and tell me that it doesn't make you expect something *special*:

Tesla Print Campaign[26]

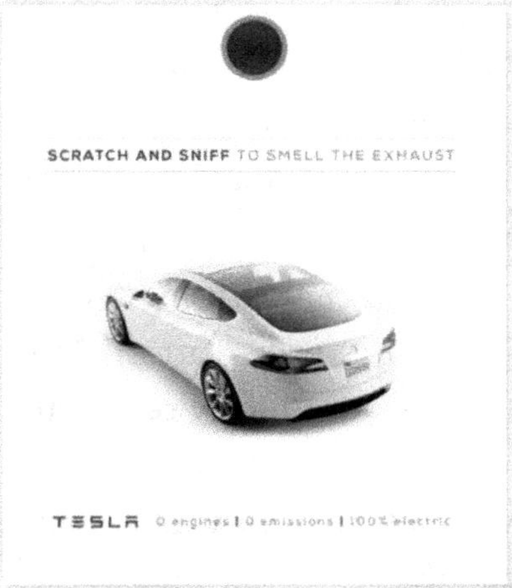
SCRATCH AND SNIFF TO SMELL THE EXHAUST
0 engines | 0 emissions | 100% electric

LIFT TO FEEL THE WEIGHT OF THE TANK
0 engines | 0 emissions | 100% electric

PRESS TO HEAR THE MOTOR START
0 engines | 0 emissions | 100% electric

Notice what the ads *don't* do: they don't state rational, informative propositions like "Tesla is quiet," "Tesla has no gas tank," or "Tesla has no exhaust smell"—factual, yet very boring. Instead, they create something you simply cannot resist; they create an *experience* that uplifts you even before you touch or test-drive a single car. How did they do that?

One technique we see in play here is Priming using sensory words ("hear," "feel," "smell") and action words ("press," "lift," "scratch and sniff") to land you solidly in your bodily senses and invite you to physically experience the attributes of the car in your sensory imagination. You can now expect, with very little doubt, that Tesla will deliver on these attributes.

Also, notice that these attributes are experiences in themselves: the sound of a car motor coming to life, lightness versus heaviness, clean air versus smelly exhaust. Remember, these elements aren't features or specs. The features, the straightforward facts that will make the rational mind an ally in creating positive expectations—"0 engines/0 emissions/100% electric"—are present, of course, but they take up a startlingly small amount of real estate at the very bottom of the ads in the self-effacing 8-point gray text.

Notice, as well, this campaign's use of Priming through the emphatic placement of bright red in these otherwise almost monochromatic ads. Red is the color that gives an edge to any football team or Olympic fighter that wears it. As the brand name is repeatedly paired with red's innate power and excitement, Priming steps in and links that power and excitement with the brand, itself. A strong desire is being built, well beneath your threshold of perception, to experience the thrill of driving a Tesla. The great performance, at this point, is taken for granted.

You may never realize it consciously but Priming through Tesla's use of the color red for its logo and copy subliminally delivers an irrational Expectation of power and excitement while driving their cars.

Priming is not the only purpose served by the recurring placement of these similar ads. Remember the Familiarity Heuristic? As customers repeatedly see the Tesla name, the Tesla image, and even the distinctive Tesla font, those things become increasingly familiar and are thus more likely to be preferred.

THE MARKETING STRATEGY IS YOU!

Perhaps no one masters performance Expectation better than Amazon and Netflix. And they do that, brilliantly, by using us, their customers, as the Priming stimuli.

Think about the last time you went to Netflix in search for a movie or a series to binge-watch. You were immediately presented with a list of options based on your previous selections. These are predictions of what you'd enjoy watching based on your previous viewing experiences. In other words, Netflix is using you to Prime you for your next selection, assuming, with a great deal of certainty, that because you liked a certain title, you're likely to enjoy the options offered in the same or a similar genre. Not only that, you now *expect* that any of the presented options will be a good choice.

To illustrate my point, here is a screenshot from my most recent visit to Netflix.

Netflix's recommendation engine uses my experience of watching *Chef's Table: France* to Prime my next viewing choice. Is it effective at getting me to select one of their presented options?

Apparently so. According to Netflix, 75% of the content watched on the service comes from its recommendation engine[27].

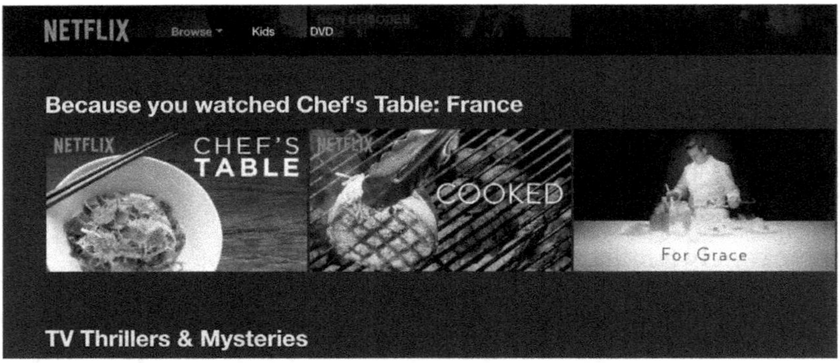

Amazon uses similar Priming and Expectation-inducing techniques. Choose an item—any item—and you're immediately offered additional items purchased by other people who also purchased the item you just have. Based on this effective Priming, you develop a strong sense of Expectation that the items offered to you by Amazon will be good complementary choices, and you add them to your cart.

Book recommendations are presented in a similar manner. Go to any book page, and beneath that book's description you'll see a headline reading, "Customers who viewed this item also viewed," followed by a list of several similar books. The implication is that if you like this book, or if you're looking for a similar book, here are ones you should consider. Amazon even tells you, "What other items do customers buy after viewing this item?" just to give you a further nudge.

Here is a screenshot of what my random search on Amazon for a book on branding brought up. Looks familiar?

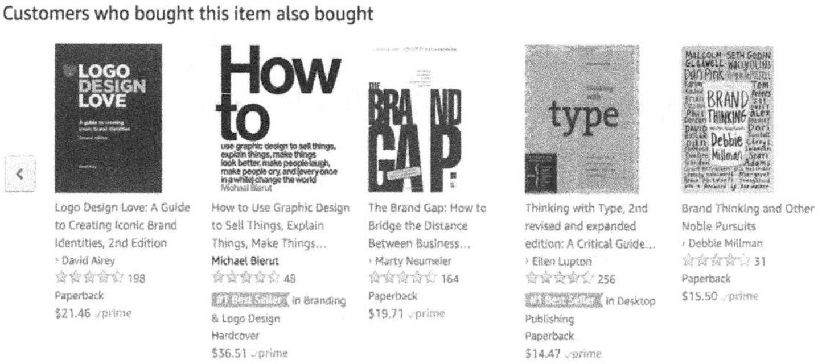

Notice, also, the star rating below each item. Star rating is the number one factor used by consumers to judge a book[28] or a business. According to a survey conducted by Dimensional Research, an overwhelming 90% of respondents who recalled reading online reviews claimed that positive reviews influenced their buying decisions, while 86% said that their buying decisions were similarly influenced by negative online reviews[29].

When you think about it from the BRAND*cebo* perspective, the mere appearance of star ratings act as a strong Priming factor (you are Conditioned to believe in the accuracy and trustworthiness of the review); your interpretation of the ratings creates a performance Expectation (five stars = great performance; one star = poor performance). And that is before you even touch the product.

HOW TO BRAND*cebo* EXPECTATIONS?

1. Create new aspirations in your audience's mind.
2. Make your brand intangibles tangible. Even if only cognitively tangible.
3. Give them a reason to expect great performance. Use statistics and success stories.
4. Align your brand promise with your audience's life goals.
5. Hype, but be truthful. False promises WILL backfire.

YOU'VE GOT TO WANT IT

So, are we all slaves to manipulative marketing designed to lead us by the nose whichever way the marketers choose? Have we forfeited the power of choice to the lure of monetary benefit through modern marketing? Although it's true that expectations can lead to wanted and unwanted consequences, there is ample research that shows Expectation, alone, might not be effective enough. It might work partially, or work for a brief period of time, but that's not what we're looking for with the BRAND*cebo* effect. We want something that genuinely enhances people's performances, lives or lifestyles as a result of using our products and services. The question then arises: how can we build our BRAND*cebo* effect to deliver on those expectations?

A third contributing factor exists for creating an effective, powerful, and meaningful placebo effect, and I discuss that in my next chapter.

Chapter 6

Desire: Mirror, Mirror On the Wall

How Consumers Self-Express Through Brand Choices

I don't play golf. Well, except once every few years when I'm asked to participate in a round for different charitable causes. And, "participate in a round" is also a bit of an overstatement. Forget about birdies or bogies, I'm elated when my club simply makes any contact with the ball. But, for true golfers, golf is a very emotional game. I learned this years ago when I was involved in developing an ad campaign for Lamkin Grips.

Shortly after I started Ameba, I was hired by one of the largest ad agencies in San Diego (at the time) to provide market and consumer insights, upon which an ad campaign would be developed for Lamkin. Lamkin Grips is one of the world's largest grip manufacturers, second only to Golf Pride (a far second, but still second!). The campaign's overarching goal was to shrink the market-share gap with Golf Pride by creating top-of-mind association between Lamkin and grips.

So, we were off to collect market and consumer insights. We started by conducting focus groups with avid golfers (playing more than 25 rounds per year) in a few cities across America. We talked about the love for the game, the role golf plays in their lives, their deep desire to constantly improve their performance, and grips.

It was astonishing though, for me and for them, that despite grips being the only physical point of contact between the player and the game (the club), they're largely ignored. In fact, players readily admitted that the hour and a half we spent talking about grips is perhaps more than they have spent thinking about them since they started playing golf. Yet, as they reflected on it, they acknowledged that they do feel a bit less confident when the grip is slippery, and their performance probably suffers when the grip is too thick, too thin, or simply uncomfortable.

As we set out to develop the campaign strategy, we were guided by two key learnings:

1. Every avid golfer, professional or amateur, carries that deep desire to hit that perfect shot one more time. And then once more. And once more...
2. Grips are mostly an afterthought. But, as the only physical point of contact between the player and the club, they directly impact performance.

The agency's creative team came out with a brilliant idea to marry the two. During that time, Nike ran a popular TV campaign (created by Wieden & Kennedy) called "I Am Tiger Woods," featuring kids aspiring to become the legendary golfer. Our Lamkin's spot parodied this commercial by showing novice golfers hitting balls off the field and into trees, frustratingly exclaiming "I Am in The Woods," then closed with a perfect swing and solution tagline: "Change your grip. Change your game."

The rationale behind this campaign's strategy reflects every step of the BRAND*cebo* model. By using humor, we injected some comic relief into an industry desperately in need of some. This was a Priming technique that immediately built brand affinity and trust: Lamkin understands golfers' deep frustrations. Then, by merely insinuating an association with Tiger Woods (it just happened that 'woods' is both a popular name and a common golf term) we created an Expectation for quality and high performance. And, finally, the perfect swing with "Change your grip. Change your game," hit that passionate Desire to experience a similar moment.

The campaign was hugely successful. Sales rose, and market share increased. It created an immediate buzz not only for Lamkin Grips, but also for the agency, with CNN, The Wall Street Journal, The New York Times and many other leading media covering the campaign's unique parody concept.

Desire—our innate motivation to be better, to feel better, to perform better—is the third and final element of the placebo effect, which completes the Brand*cebo* equation:

Priming + Expectation + Desire = BRAND*cebo*.

As a child, I was incredibly motivated to become a better soccer player. I wanted to be better than my peers and imagined, with great Desire, becoming a soccer superstar. Parents who bought Tiny Love or Baby Einstein toys were motivated to see their children develop in the best way possible—a Desire shared by all parents. In my dissertation study, the kids demonstrated their innate motivation to run faster in a high-performance shoe that boasted that desirable swoosh.

So now, let's take a close look at the various aspects of the Desire element of the placebo effect.

DESIRE AND SELF-IMAGE

Much of our self-image is based on what others think of us. We want to look good in the eyes of the right people. Well-designed brands help individuals feel like they have gained acceptance from others. That's what makes people "label conscious." If the cool people are wearing Diesel jeans and you also wear them that, by default, makes you much closer to being a cool person. The brand becomes an extension of the wearers' personalities.

The next step up, however, is creating a higher level of consumer-brand relationships. From a brand being a symbol for social status ("I'm wearing Prada, so people will think that I'm successful") to a brand being an aspect of self-actualization, ("I'm wearing Prada, because it makes *me* feel more confident.") This is the core of the BRAND*cebo* effect: when you actually feel better about yourself, without regard for what others think, the full effect of the placebo kicks in and you actually *are* better: physiologically, emotionally, and mentally.

Studies have shown that men who buy expensive suits before an important interview perform better in the interview[1]. I played better soccer, pregnant women with morning sickness felt better, and kids actually ran faster due to the BRAND*cebo* effect.

It takes a great deal of intimacy with a brand to achieve that state—an intimacy as great as in any deep relationship. The closer and more harmonious the relationship between a person's self-image and the image the brand presents, the more likely that person is to buy the product.

The *Self-Expansion Theory*[2] states that a basic human desire is to grow: intellectually, emotionally, financially, etc. This growth is achieved through close and trusted relationships, and affects a person's self-image and sense of personal value.

This theory also applies to brands and their degree of intimacy. As people develop an affinity for a brand, they experience emotional arousal and an identity lift. Think about Cartier, Nike, or Starbucks. People who love Cartier wear their new bracelet and feel more beautiful, more special, and more powerful. The latest Nike shoes with the highest ratings, given the strong degree of intimacy and trust, will actually make people who love Nike run faster—measurably faster. And that Starbucks coffee? All is needed is to see the logo and fans of the brand automatically feel better about life and themselves.

A MOST POWERFUL UNION

According to some researchers, Desire and Expectation are almost inseparable, and the two of them combine to create a more powerful state: that of hope[3]. 'Hope,' in this context, doesn't necessarily mean expecting that events will turn out fine, but rather that they'll make sense.

For example, if you're being treated for a medical issue, you certainly have an Expectation and Desire for your treatment to work. In branding, this powerful union also applies. We have an Expectation and Desire that a prestigious brand or higher-priced product will outperform their lower-priced and lesser-branded competitors. It simply makes sense to us that this should be the case, and so it is. Our natural motivation is for the product to provide better performance in order justify the higher price we paid.

We can ask if the über-efficacy of the higher-priced product comes from our Expectation that higher prices predict higher quality. And we can ask if, perhaps, instead it comes from our

Desire to rationalize the higher-priced product to have the purchase make sense in our world.

The fact remains that the two may be tangled in our minds and hearts; Desire combined with Expectation creates one powerful placebo, indeed.

DISTILLING DESIRE FROM EXPECTATION

In an attempt to separate the efficacy of Desire from Expectation, researchers conducted additional studies on the basic-energy-drink-versus-price study[4].

They divided 106 undergraduate students into three groups. One group was given the actual energy drink, a second was given a placebo energy drink (a non-caffeinated drink that tasted like the actual energy drink), while the third group was given an ordinary glass of water.

Each participant was given promotional material to read regarding the wonders of the energy drink. A can of the drink, bearing its logo and brand message, was placed at the front of each testing room. Participants were asked questions to determine their actual Desire for the drink to work and their expectations of whether it would improve their stamina or mood. Desire and Expectation were identified and separated.

Finally, participants' blood pressure, overall energy level, mental alertness, and physical reflexes were all measured before imbibing the energy drink. After consuming their respective drinks, participants were physically tested again.

The results clearly showed that placebo-drinking participants who had high motivation for the drink to work experienced a heightened physical state[5]. However, those with a low Expectation for the drink to work experienced no physiological changes.

The researchers concluded that Desire is a key component of the placebo effect. *Wanting* something to work is important.

THE POWER OF DESIRE

Let's look at the flipside: is it possible for the placebo effect to work even when we *don't* want it to work? In Chapter 2, I introduced the concept of the *nocebo* effect in which the placebo effect causes a negative outcome. This was demonstrated through the *golem* effect: having low expectations of someone leads to that person meeting those low expectations. The voodoo deaths also demonstrated that people who believed they were going to die because of a cast spell did, indeed, die.

It turns out that the nocebo effect may be more pervasive than we realize. Think back to the last time you zoned out in front of the TV. Perhaps it was one recent evening or a rainy weekend day. You were watching golf, football, or your favorite cooking show. On came a commercial for some kind of medicine; maybe it promised to lower high blood pressure, correct erectile dysfunction, or end that sneezing-coughing-sore throat. Remember how the commercial ended? With a list of potential side effects so long you wondered why they made the drug in the first place.

Rebecca Erwin Wells and Ted Kaptchuk published an article in *The American Journal of Bioethics* entitled, "To Tell the Truth, the Whole Truth, May Do Patients Harm: The Problem of the Placebo Effect for Informed Consent[6]." The article discussed researchers who found that citing detailed lists of possible side effects actually increased the chances of having one of the named side effects. "Evidence suggests that the nocebo effect can significantly increase various nonspecific symptoms and complaints, resulting in psychological distress, significant excess costs because of increased medication non-adherence, extra treatment visits, and additional medicines prescribed to treat the nocebo effects[7]."

Informed consent has all the correct ethics attached in that doctors must make sure their patients understand the risks involved in any medication or treatment prescribed. Well of course, you say: That's the right thing to do. And it is. Until it isn't. It may, in fact, do more harm than good because of the nocebo effect.

Drug trials aren't the only place the nocebo effect occurs. Just hearing negative gossip or beliefs is enough to affect someone not just mentally but physiologically, as well. Brain scans of people experiencing nocebo suggestions, such as in the example about negative side effects, result in increased activity in the hypothalmus, the pituitary gland, and the adrenal gland[8]. These areas are responsible for much of the flight or fight action we experience in response to danger.

"Negative expectations can be communicated to your friends, neighbors, and the like, and they spread very quickly, producing social nocebo effects in a large population of subjects," said Fabrizio Benedetti at the University of Turin Medical School[9]. It would seem that Priming and Expectation can work against, or without, Desire and still win.

Well, maybe.

There are two ways of looking at this nocebo motivational conundrum. You listen diligently to your doctor explaining the possible side effects of your medication. Consciously, you certainly don't want an unexpected ugly rash on your foot. You have a distinct *lack* of motivation to experience that result.

However, after being told by someone you respect and believe (the doctor) that it could be a side effect, you actually develop the rash. Could it be that part of you wanted the doctor to be right? A white-coat-clad professional brings order into a world of chaos, so in a roundabout way, his warning could have become a subconscious motivational factor to develop the rash.

I'll let you decide, but suffice it to say, the mind and body are inextricably linked in complex and myriad ways. And for the purpose of this book and the BRAND*cebo* effect, when we're motivated for a certain outcome to occur, it makes it more likely that it will happen.

IT'S JUST A PEN, RIGHT?

I recently pitched an international corporate promotion company that manufactures pens—millions and millions of them. For example, when you go into the auto body shop to get the ding taken out of your fender, they hand you a pen with their name and address on it, just as your financial advisor or CPA do.

My prospective client knew that, statistically, they should get approximately 1.5% response from pen marketing, so if they sent out one million pens, they would expect 15,000 orders. Nobody cares much about the custom pen manufacturer, itself, as they provide such an unassuming, low-key product. But along comes their 50th anniversary, and they want to take advantage of this remarkable occasion. Many of their clients had been around for decades; many were father-to-son or family-style businesses, which is their target market.

In the process of developing the campaign, we came up with the slogan, "*Every great legacy starts at the tip of a pen.*" It began as a story about business, but now it's an emotional story. We gathered stories of small businesses that had survived the ups and downs of businesses that were passed on from generation to generation. In so doing, the business created a legacy, and we wanted to remind them that the pen company was along with them every step of the way.

Much like Lampkin's "Change your grip. Change your game." campaign, this example tapped into the three elements of the placebo effect and tied them all together with a strong and emotional message. We Primed the viewer to the pervasiveness of the promotional company through the life of their business. The viewer, then, came to expect the pens to reflect their own company's history and story. And the viewer was motivated to buy more pens because they saw their own story—themselves—in the product.

BUILDING BRAND*cebo*
Step 3: From Interest to Desire

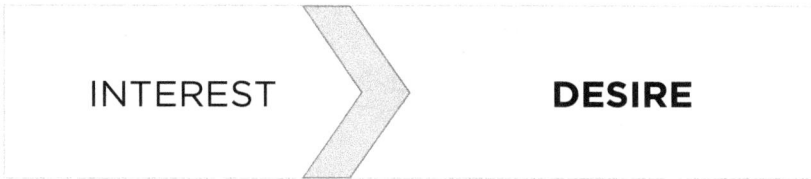

INTEREST ❯ **DESIRE**

The final step and ultimate goal of any traditional brand development campaign is creating brand interest. This is achieved once a company has skillfully shaped brand awareness into positive brand perception through messages and positive experiences that engage both the rational and irrational sides of consumers' buying behaviors. Yet just like awareness and perception, interest is mainly a result of an analytical process that is greatly affected by cost vs. benefit calculations.

Desire adds a heavy emotional layer to this process and allows our hearts and guts to become powerful influencers on our decisions. In the BRAND*cebo* context, Desire is more than simply what we want. It is much deeper. It is what we want *to be.* It reflects our inner motivation to excel, to grow, to self-actualize. And we naturally gravitate towards people, careers, lifestyles...and brands that enable our aspirations.

Here's an example from my own life. I met my cousin for dinner on a recent trip to London. My cousin asked about my research into the placebo effect of brands. I told her what I'd learned, but she was not convinced. She challenged me with her conviction that "good brands actually *do* last longer."

"Do they actually *last* longer, or do we *keep* them longer because they are good brands?" I asked. She thought about it, laughed, and conceded the point.

Think of your own closet. How many items in there are way past their prime but are still hanging on because "they are good brands"? I have some old Dior dress shoes that, if the government required an expiration date for shoes, would now be extinct. I've thrown away many newer, better-looking shoes over the years but not my Diors.

But better looking is not the point. The point is that what people might look at as old shoes look practically new to me. I don't see the aged leather. To me they look as beautiful as they were the day I bought them, and when I wear them, I believe that with them I am lookin' *good*.

BRAND*cebo* effect? Probably, but no less real for it. As we do with wine, cars, energy drinks, sunglasses, and cashmere sweaters, we apply to and actually *experience* higher quality attributes with desirable brands. A "lesser" brand would not have *lasted* that long in my closet. Not figuratively: literally.

In the study about women wearing shawls labeled or not labeled Hermes, the women who believed they were wearing a Hermes-branded shawl actually experienced a higher body temperature than the women who wore the same shawl but unlabeled. Naturally, both groups of women were motivated to be warm. Yet in the Hermes group, that Desire went deeper. It was not simply the need to get warmer, but the Desire for the Hermes brand to perform better, an innate motivation to justify and satisfy their Primed belief and aspirational Expectation that it undoubtedly would. And it did.

Think back to the energy drink example. When participants drank what they believed to be the higher-priced energy drink, they physiologically experienced a more alert and invigorated state. However when they were informed of the deceit that they had, in fact, drunk a lower-priced drink, the placebo effect weakened significantly. They clearly expected that a higher-priced drink would create a better result than the cheap alternative. You get what you pay for.

But it is not Expectation, alone. Seen from the motivational theorist perspective, participants' declined performance following the reveal was due to their Desire to justify the higher-priced drink. If you pay more, you *want* (not just expect) it to work better.

So the inner Desire to be better can be ignited by brands (through Priming and Expectation building); in return, consumers impart that Desire upon the brand, creating their own disposition for it to perform.

The Brand Desire Exchange[10]

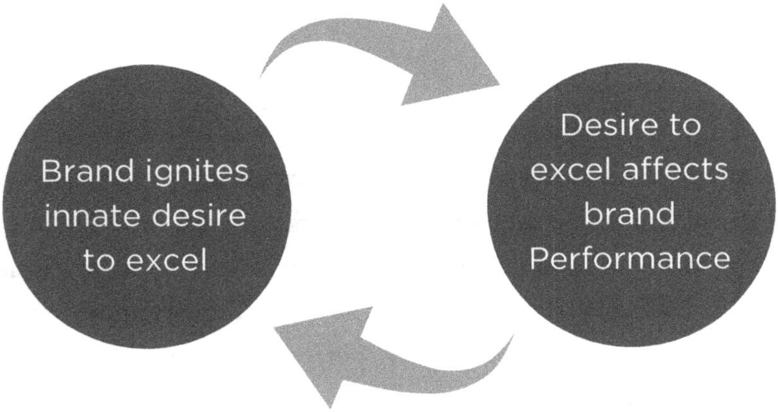
Brand ignites innate desire to excel
Desire to excel affects brand Performance

In my study of the BRAND*cebo* effect of Nike, prior to using the branded running shoes, I presented the youngsters with a questionnaire regarding their motivation to excel with the Nike brand. The questionnaire included two simple questions:

1. How much would you like this pair of Nike® Free Run 5.0 shoes to improve your running speed?

Not at all				Very much
1	2	3	4	5

2. How much would you like this pair of Nike® Free Run 5.0 shoes to help you win the race?

Not at all				Very much
1	2	3	4	5

Findings conclusively demonstrated the correlation between consumer motivation and brand performance. Participants who expressed increased motivation to run faster with the Nike brand did, in fact, run faster. Conversely, participants who were Primed for the Nike brand but believed they would be running with a lesser brand expressed a low performance motivation and experienced worse performance.

These young runners who had been exposed (Primed) to the superiority of the Nike running shoes and developed the Expectation to perform better in the 50-meter run, combined their Desire to run faster than their peers with their Desire for the brand to perform true to their Expectation, and so it did.

HOW TO BRAND*cebo* DESIRE?

1. Everyone wants to be better (know better, feel better, perform better). Show how your brand could help.
2. Identify your audience's desired personal and lifestyle destination. Believe in it.
3. Clearly align your brand with your audience's desired destination.
4. Make your brand promises aspirational, desirable, and tangible.
5. Tightly align your brand values and attributes with the personal values and beliefs of your audience. You know you've arrived when they can see themselves in your brand, and express themselves through it.

A LITTLE KNOWN DISCOVERY

We now understand the three key elements necessary to create the most powerful placebo and, therefore, BRAND*cebo*, effect. But in my study, I also came upon a phenomenon of which there's almost no academic study. The placebo effect doesn't affect only the people involved with the product or service; it also affects those people using other brands. I have called this the *Ricochet Effect,* and I cover it in the next chapter.

Understanding and exploiting the Ricochet Effect can have a direct impact on how your branding message will create the most powerful BRAND*cebo.*

Chapter 7

The Ricochet Effect

How Desirable Brands Directly Affect Product Performance of Competitive Brands

Over the past three chapters, I've extensively discussed the three pivotal elements that give the placebo effect so much power. Priming, Expectation, and Desire create the placebo effect, either alone or most effectively when combined.

But these three elements don't have only direct effects; they have indirect ones, too. Sometimes these indirect effects are intentional, and sometimes they're not.

The most surprising element that came from my running-shoe experiment was the ability of a powerful brand to negatively affect the performance of a competing brand. And by "negatively affect," I don't just mean give an inferior impression; I mean create real and measurable inferior performance results. To my knowledge, this is the first time this effect has been studied in the context of branding. The importance of this cannot be overstated due to the powerful branding effects inherent in BRAND*cebo*.

We're all probably aware of the classic spillover effect in brands. An unknown brand immediately gets a brand boost when placed on the shelf next to a well-known, luxury brand. Similarly, a well-known brand will leverage the spillover effect when launching a new product. Rather than spending time and money creating awareness and garnering respect for the new product, the company simply advertises it in context with their already well-known and respected product as a brand extension.

For example, a popular face lotion brand might launch a special anti-aging cream. They can quickly leverage the current brand awareness and loyalty by advertising the new cream in the context of the current and widely popular product.

How about celebrity endorsements? If you pick up a business book bearing a glowing endorsement by Bill Gates on the front cover, his already established brand value—knowledge, success, and expertise—will spill over onto the brand of that book, making consumers more likely to buy it.

The Ricochet Effect, however, is different. This is where the positive perception of one brand leads to a corresponding negative perception and performance of another brand.

Let's say you love a certain brand of handbag, but a friend comes by with a different brand and you learn it is the hottest brand around. Everyone who's anyone has that brand. If you develop a negative and inferior perception of your own handbag because of this information, you're experiencing the Ricochet Effect.

These two different yet powerful side effects of a strong brand raise fascinating questions. Is it possible that the Desire for a specific brand could have a negative impact on the actual performance—not just perception, but performance—of a competing brand? My research would say yes. The kids who ran wearing the "inferior" brand performed measurably worse than those kids wearing the "superior" brand. This is all we can say conclusively, but if this Ricochet Effect exists, how else could it be playing out in our lives?

In my personal soccer story, I wrote how I not only became a better player, but because my opponents heard me being called either Cruyff or Beckenbauer, their play actually worsened. They hadn't picked up any bad techniques or had faulty equipment or injuries. All they had was the Priming and Expectation that I would play better, which caused them to play more poorly.

Other than my study with kids and running shoes, all we have as evidence of the Ricochet Effect are questions and assumptions. But what interesting questions, indeed. Just as the placebo effect has been playing out in our lives largely unnoticed for centuries, could the same be true for the Ricochet Effect? And what does this mean for the power of the BRAND*cebo* effect?

Below are several examples of what could be the Ricochet Effect in various aspects of life.

Lacking any further scientific evidence, decide for yourself what's happening in the mysterious world of the human psyche.

THE DIETING DILEMMA

Let's take dieting. When we begin a diet, we have all three of the essential placebo effect elements in place. We believe the diet will work because we've been given the necessary Priming stimuli that it should. Maybe there is scientific evidence that eating strawberries and kale for months on end burns fat. Or a celebrity swears they lost 95 pounds by following this diet. Therefore, we have been Primed; we Expect the diet to work because we have seen it work for others. And we certainly Desire for it to work because we want to lose weight.

But along comes a new, trendy diet that a credible batch of scientists and/or celebrities claim is the most effective diet, ever. We need to ask: Could the Ricochet Effect come into play here and be part of the reason why most diets don't work? Most diets work for a while, and then they don't. There are different explanations for this. Could one part of the mystery be that there's a better "brand" in town, and if we're still working with the "inferior" brand, then it begins to underperform physiologically? This would be the Ricochet Effect in action.

WHOM YOU SIT NEXT TO MATTERS

Many teachers from elementary level through high school and into the highest levels of college experience at least an equivalent to the Ricochet Effect in their very own classrooms.

For example, a 2008 study of students from grades three through ten demonstrated that having higher-ranking (better performing) and lower-ranking students in the same class affect each other's performance[1]. Specifically, at each grade level, the lowest-ranked students in the class improved their math and reading scores *by almost an entire grade level* when higher-ranking students were added to the class. The lower-ranked students hadn't been given extra homework or attention that they wouldn't ordinarily have received; simply the presence of these higher-performing students made the difference.

However, a negative Ricochet Effect also occurred. It seems that the ratio of high- to low-ranking students matters. When the class contained a greater percentage of lower-ranking students, the higher-ranked students suffered significant declines in their math and reading scores. The Ricochet Effect at work?

Interestingly, gender also matters. It's been shown that when girls make up more than 50% of a class, the boys experience an average 2.3% increase in their test scores[2]. As in the example above, the boys weren't given any extra instruction, support materials, or attention. The only change was the mix of the students, which had the indirect effect of raising the boys' test scores.

RICOCHET IN THE FIELD OF SPORTS

The Ricochet Effect might be more ubiquitous in the world of sports than we realize. When an NBA basketball team includes a "superstar" player, on average the offensive performance of each player improves considerably (as measured by total points, successful shooting percentage, and number of assists)[3]. Interestingly, the star power present doesn't improve free-throw statistics[4]. Researchers believe that this is because the player stands for his free throw shot individually so the team Ricochet Effect is less significant.

Conventional wisdom in baseball believe that, even though it is a team sport, the Ricochet Effect won't occur because each player is evaluated individually (as above with free throws) and a baseball team's performance is nothing more than a sum of its individual players' performances[5]. However, more recent studies prove this isn't always the case.

Researchers in 2008 studied earned run averages (ERA) and batting averages of players from 1953 through 2003. Utilizing regression analysis, they concluded that individual pitcher and batter performance was significantly influenced by the spillover from teammates' performances[6]. If their fellow team members played well, then batters achieved higher batting averages, and pitchers posted lower ERAs. One has to wonder if the opposite holds true as well: individuals perform more poorly when fellow team members also perform poorly.

Baseball provides yet another conundrum in that fans have long held the belief in "protection"—that being preceded by a good batter will improve the batting of the next batter, while being preceded by a bad batter will negatively affect the next batter[7]. This is apparently a variation on the Ricochet Effect.

Instead, researchers studying the performances of Major League Baseball players found a *negative* correlation between the current batter and his on-deck teammates' performance[8]. If the current batter performed well, the on-deck hitter performed more poorly. They went on to state that this performance link then affected the strategy of the opposing pitcher and thereby, his ultimate performance, too. This study begs the question: Is this some variation on the Ricochet Effect? And if so, what underlies it?

THE RICOCHET EFFECT AND...THE OSCARS?

Believe it or not, researchers have even applied the spillover effect to the Oscars. In a 2010 study, scientists created a massive database of the top-ten-credited movie roles between 1936 and 2005[9]. The data they drew from included nearly 150,000 performances by over 37,000 actors in over 16,000 films.

The results were conclusive: 1) actors with similar experience (years in the business, type of roles played) had a higher chance of being nominated if they performed with high-caliber co-stars; and 2) unknown actors' chances of being nominated increased by a whopping 35% if they collaborated with previous Oscar-winning talent[10]. High-level star power spilled over into their lesser known and less experienced co-stars.

To see possible evidence of this, we only have to look back as far as the 2016 Oscars. Mark Rylance played a supporting role in Bridge of Spies in which Tom Hanks had the starring role. Rylance won Best Supporting Actor for a Supporting Role even though it was his first time nominated. Alicia Vikander won Best Supporting Actress for her role in *The Danish Girl* opposite Eddie Redmayne, a much more experienced and successful actor. In fact, the previous year, Redmayne had won Best Actor for his role in *The Theory of Everything*, a memoir of Stephen Hawking.

Is this evidence of the positive side of the Ricochet Effect? It's up to you to decide.

THE UPGRADE DOWNSIDE

A fascinating area of consideration of a potential Ricochet Effect is within product upgrades. For example, I eagerly awaited the launch of iPhone (as of this writing, the latest iPhone iteration). Until the day Apple announced the anticipated release of the iPhone, I was perfectly happy with my iPhone 7. It was fast and efficient, easy to use, and the phone's camera was decent enough. But since the announcement, I suddenly feel that my iPhone 7 was never really that good. Surely its pictures are less sharp than I expect, it is slower and feels kind of clumsy, and the battery life is becoming a source of constant frustration. All of these feelings come over me, and I haven't even seen the iPhone yet.

Because I am Primed to believe that the new iPhone will be better, I expect it to be so. And because I will surely pay a premium to put my hands on one as soon as it is released, I am highly motivated for it to be better than any smart phone on the market. As you know by now, all of these factors equate to the BRAND*cebo* effect in the new phone and the Ricochet Effect in the old phone.

The same could hold true for any upgrade, whether it's the new model of Toyota you just bought, a software upgrade, or even a new online game. You have all the ingredients of the placebo effect in place. Would that not lead to a natural lowering of your perception of the item being replaced? The Ricochet Effect could be alive and well every time we update a product or service, and all without our even noticing it.

Entire libraries could be filled with books deciphering consumers' buying behaviors. After all, discovering the key to what makes consumers choose one product over another would be any company's dream.

IT'S NOT JUST CHILD'S PLAY

Over $20 billion is spent in the United States each year on toys. Child's play is big business.

Periodically, a toy production proves dangerous or faulty, and is therefore recalled. The more highly publicized these recalls, the more immediately damaging they are to the overall sales of brands in the same category of toys, even after the flaw is corrected. But it doesn't stop there. Studies have shown that recalls affect the sales of *all the other* toys in that category, be it action figures, dolls, or board games and puzzles[11]. Category sales could drop by as much as 30%, which is clear evidence of the Ricochet Effect. Perfectly safe, well-functioning toys are *not* bought because one of their plastic kin was recalled. And sales dropped across all toy companies, not just the one experiencing the recall.

This Ricochet Effect was caused by consumers adjusting their perception of, and therefore buying behavior regarding, the safety and quality of *all toys* in that category.

THE DOMINO EFFECT

We can clearly see from the above example that the Ricochet Effect causes a sort of domino effect. It wasn't just the original toy maker's company that suffered diminished sales, but all toy companies that sold that category of toys. Media messages about one product can affect the sales of a similar product at a completely different company.

Recently, Volkswagen, the car manufacturer, got into deep trouble after reports aired about it having rigged emission tests. The company not only took a financial hit due to legal fees, class actions suits, and even a criminal investigation, but it also suffered a huge drop in future sales of its cars. None of this is surprising.

However, the interesting part, from our perspective, is that sales and share prices also dropped for other German-based automakers, specifically Daimler and BMW. They weren't found guilty and subject to fines and investigations; they were innocent bystanders, so to speak. But nonetheless, their sales were hit due to their perceived proximity (simply by being in the same industry) to Volkswagon.

RICOCHET AND FIRST IMPRESSIONS

A recent psychological study found that when men were exposed to pictures of overly sexualized women (minimally dressed, excessively made up, etc.), it affected how they viewed all women. The men rated the scantily clad women as less intelligent and having poor morality[12]. This perception spilled over into the next study in which the same men were asked to rate modestly dressed women who were physically present at the study site. The men rated these women as less intelligent and less moral, too, even though they were actual study participants. Based on what we know of the Ricochet Effect, this could certainly be part of the explanation.

WHAT'S IN A RICOCHET EFFECT?

So what is the Ricochet Effect? What elements does it have, and how can we better understand them? To answer these questions, researchers Mas and Moretti demonstrated that low-performing store cashiers exhibited significant improvement in productivity when they were paired with high-performing cashiers[13], much as we saw in the changes in performance of low-ranking students in classes with high-ranking students. Based on this evidence, Mas and Moretti arrived at three key factors that lead to a Ricochet Effect:

1. Social pressure (much like motivation): If you're around people whose performance (academically, athletically, etc.) is better than your own, you are motivated to improve.
2. Prosocial preferences: A cashier might feel competitive and Desire to improve his or her skills or might want to avoid the guilt associated with underperforming.
3. Knowledge spillover: The higher-skilled cashiers either consciously transmitted information to help the lower-skilled cashiers or they subconsciously inspired their co-workers to acquire more knowledge.

Can we assume that the inverse holds true for the negative Ricochet Effect? Are you demotivated if surrounded by people whose performance is worse than your own? Is low-performance-based guilt eliminated when there is less competition? Is there less knowledge to go around and therefore people perform more poorly?

Other researchers have attributed the Ricochet Effect to a phenomenon called the *Associated Learning Model*[14]. According to this model, any sign or stimulus that helps people forecast an outcome is considered predictive. Therefore, individuals learn to predict outcomes based on the presence of different stimuli. Ultimately, this creates the Ricochet Effect.

While there are likely even more factors involved in the creation of the Ricochet Effect, we know one thing for sure: just as the placebo effect creates real, physiological outcomes, so does the Ricochet Effect. It's just as real and possibly as powerful as the placebo effect.

PUTTING IT ALL TOGETHER

The premise of this book is that a plethora of information and perceptions are constantly being processed in the deepest corners of our minds that we may or may not be aware of. Through the placebo effect, we know that we can be physiologically affected based on the Priming, Expectation, and Desire around a brand. We can also experience a Ricochet Effect when we use an "inferior" brand as it may degrade our performance on a physiological level.

What does this all mean when it comes to branding? How can we combine all this information and act upon, or at least understand, relevant and timely conclusions? In the final chapter, The BRAND*cebo* effect, we'll see what happens when we put it all together.

Chapter 8

Building BRAND*cebo*

How to Transform Brand Loyalty into Enriching Brand Dependency

In previous chapters, we established that through the three elements of the placebo effect, powerful brands have distinct and beneficial physiological effects on consumers; in short, their products work better. This BRAND*cebo* effect has been solidly demonstrated across a wide range of products, from running shoes, to wines and energy drinks, and even to child development toys.

I have suggested a new brand development model that is emotionally focused and allows the audience to self-express through its attributes and values. This BRAND*cebo* model of brand development transforms the traditional brand loyalty model (Awareness—Perception—Interest) into a more thought-provoking, placebo-induced, positive brand dependency model (Priming—Expectation—Desire).

Building BRAND*cebo*[1]

Brand loyalty is the willingness of the consumer to rely on the brand to perform its stated function. Behaviorally speaking, it is a customer's tendency to stick with the same brand rather than try a competing one. Loyalty alone, though, is not enough.

As recently as 1980, 80% of U.S. car purchases were made by returning customers; by 2009, that figure had plunged to 20%[2]. By

2014, only three automakers—Toyota, Honda, and Ford—still had at least 50% return customers[3].

Furthermore, 78% of all consumers are not loyal to a particular brand[4]. The days when we could expect customers to return to us as a matter of course are behind us. New research from behavioral-marketing company Silverpop reveals that while people may still be extremely loyal to the brands they love the most, they typically have only about five of these "Best Friend" companies from which they will repeatedly open emails and buy products[5].

Where did brand loyalty go? In this world of proliferating choice, accessible alternatives, canny competition, and active consumers, the fact is that people today expect more from their brands than they used to—not just more functionality, but a more authentic emotional connection.

A national survey found that nearly half of all people between 18 and 44 years of age said that any loyalty they feel towards brands in the future will have to come from the types of experiences brands create for them[6].

Diminished customer loyalty is just a symptom of companies' failure to meet these rising emotional demands. But when, like Harley-Davidson and Starbucks, companies *do* meet these demands, they are rewarded with soaring commitment levels. In today's hyper-connected world, brands that deliver big on emotion stand head and shoulders above the crowd.

Another recent study of U.S adults asked, "How would you feel if [your favorite brand] went away or no longer existed?" Fifty-one percent of respondents said they would be "devastated[7]."

Creating BRAND*cebo*-based brand dependency does not imply malicious cognitive marketing manipulation. Quite the contrary. BRAND*cebo*-based brand dependency works only when the brand embodies consumers' values and aspirations, and its products deliver effective, meaningful, and consistently excellent performance that genuinely enhances consumers' lives or lifestyle. Consumers become brand-dependent because through that brand they are able to self-express.

BRAND*cebo*-based Brand Dependency[8]

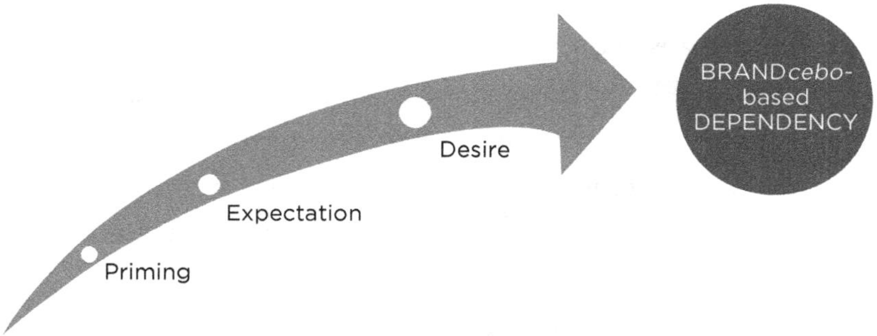

In our ultra-fast-paced consumer culture, brand loyalty could be a temporary trait. To ensure long-term consumer commitment, we need to move consumers from brand *loyalty* to brand *dependency*. Consistent with Susan Fournier's philosophy of brands as relationships, brand dependency represents a strong bond between the customer and the brand. It is a relationship characterized by trust, admiration, devotion, and even love. Through Priming and familiarity, the brand is freighted with associations that reach out to the consumer's emotions, self-image, confidence, identity, and feelings of personal worth. The brand-as-conditioned-stimulus is now in full force.

I'm not just talking about the simple satisfaction that comes when a product functions as reliably as promised. This is fundamental but not primary. When you add the kind of meaningful brand experiences we've been talking about, the brand relationship becomes deeper, more intimate, and more passionate. This kind of dependency denotes an emotional investment in the brand that would lead to an unmitigated commitment—the kind of commitment that has been defined as "an enduring desire to maintain a valued relationship[9]."

This "enduring desire" to maintain the relationship supplies motivation for it to work and succeed, and as you will recall, Desire is the third element of the placebo effect. This same Desire, born of an emotional bond with the brand, fuels what we could describe as "product overperformance." Under these circumstances, the consumer experiences functions and qualities that go beyond those promised by the brand, perceive a level of performance even higher than what the company had intended or hoped for, and feels an elevated level of brand-induced satisfaction and performance that the consumer becomes dependent upon.

Product overperformance includes physiological effects such as running faster in certain shoes, lighting up the pleasure centers of the brain when tasting inferior wine, and stamina and mood improvement powered by energy drinks—effects that further heighten positive expectations and strengthen positive Priming. These are BRAND*cebo* effects.

BRAND*cebo* Brand Performance Model[10]

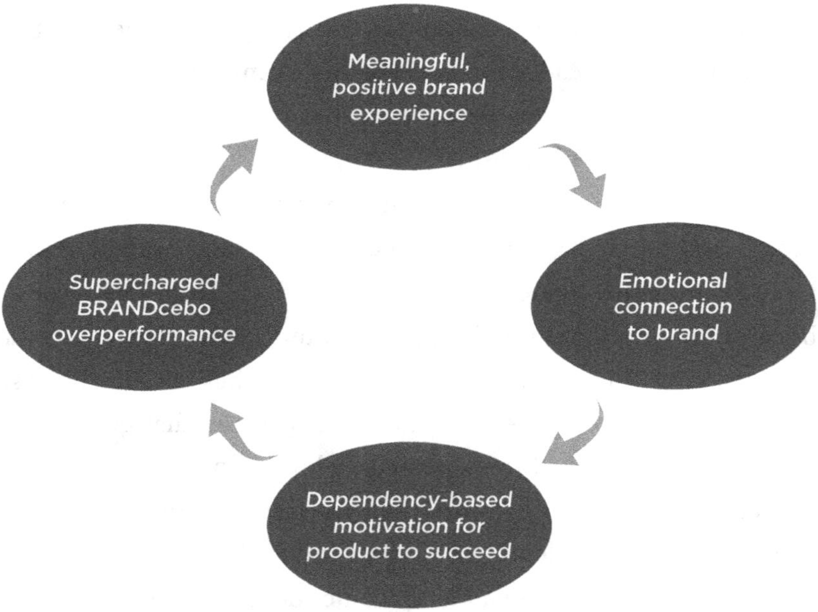

Consider, for example, my experiment with the children and the Nike running shoes. They believed so much in the superiority of the Nike brand, and were so motivated to experience that superiority, that they simply ran faster in those branded shoes. Similarly, loyal energy drink consumers are so motivated to experience the energy boost that they create for themselves the desired pick-me-up, even when the drink contains no energy-inducing elements.

But customers are not the only ones who benefit from this kind of dependency. Businesses, too, stand to profit from it.

In their commitment to their brands, brand-dependent customers are often willing to pay more for their beloved brands because they are certain, without a doubt, that it has some special value that no other alternative can offer. A repeat customer is estimated to spend 67% more than a new customer[11]. Customers who are fully engaged can deliver a 23% premium in terms of share-of-wallet, profitability, revenue, and relationship growth[12]. Engaged consumers buy 90% more often, spend about 60% more each time, and are five times more likely to say that the brand is the only one they would consider buying in the future[13]. Combined, these advantages can mean that brand-dependent customers deliver three times the value to the brand over the course of a year. Another estimate has the average profit per customer increasing between 25 and 100% if only 5% more customers can be brought into committed brand dependency[14].

Brand-dependent consumers are also more resistant to competition and more forgiving to the brand's shortfalls. Their positive word-of-mouth contributions bring in new customers and reduce marketing costs. Brand-dependent customers initiate, promote, and inspire community that, increasingly, is the currency of value in our social-media-laden world.

A great example is how Harley-Davidson's user community, now fueled by social media, has enabled the company to command more than half of the US motorcycle market with very little spending on marketing[15].

Another example of a company that consciously and successfully courts brand dependency is Starbucks. In the aggressive US coffeehouse market, which is expected to climb to $46.2 billion in revenue by 2021, Starbucks stands alone[16]. Since they opened their first store in 1971, they have achieved a remarkable 40% monthly repeat visit rate, a unique achievement even in the growing artisanal coffee movement[17]. This amazing brand dependency is not just about the coffee but about the way

Starbucks makes its customers *feel* welcome and at home in their stores. They essentially invite their customers to live there. Coffeehouses have become the official third place after home and the office[18].

What Starbucks markets is not just a drink but the experience of going to Starbucks. Customers are willing to pay a premium for this home-away-from-home feeling of belonging. The high price of Starbucks coffee is widely commented on and rises every year, but loyal customers continue to pay it gladly.

An oft-ignored example of brand dependency is patriotism or nationalism (We tend to call it "patriotism" when we feel it and "nationalism" when someone else does). Countries are super-mega brands, and are highly successful at creating intimate, irrevocable loyalty, which we call "nationality." We so self-identify with our nationality that its attributes become our own. Just saying "American," "French," "Israeli," or "Chinese" immediately conveys a perception of appearance, values, beliefs, and so forth, even if you have never actually met an American, Frenchman, Israeli, or Chinese person.

And we are not simply loyal to this brand; we pledge allegiance to it. We are so motivated to see it succeed that we are willing to pay a significant portion of our personal income for it to flourish. We defend it against perceived enemies, and in extreme cases sacrifice our lives for it.

What makes country brands so successful in creating this intense level of loyalty? Like Harley-Davidson, they create a community of individuals with shared interests and build a compelling story that instills pride within its members. This sense of pride is maintained by the exclusivity of this membership, a.k.a. "citizenship," and is nourished through ongoing and repeated messages regarding the superiority of this brand (country) and its now-dependent customers (citizens).

Brand developers striving to build effective, long-lasting, committed, and self-motivated dependency have a lot to learn from the conscious and unconscious branding elements used by countries to build nationality. This kind of brand dependency is reached when consumers fully identify themselves with the brand, and see its success as their success and its failure as their failure. And since no one likes to fail, consumers are motivated to find unique brand values and positive attributes. They experience product overperformance otherwise unrealized by other users. They experience the BRAND*cebo* effect.

As brand loyalty, in its traditional expression, becomes less meaningful, a key goal for the BRAND*cebo*-aware marketer is to build committed relationships with consumers in which loyalty is defined not only by their repeated product purchases, but by their innate Desire for the product to overperform and the brand to succeed.

NINE POINTS TO FINISH WITH

BRAND*cebo*-aware marketers need to Prime their customers to identify with and trust their brand, encourage them to Expect superior performance of its products, and nurture their Desire to self-actualize through it. To accomplish this BRAND*cebo* state, marketers must master the following principles:

1. ***Is your brand a role model?*** When a brand and its customers have the same worldview, beliefs, and intentions, the brand relationship is deeper and more intimate. Aspire for your brand to be a role model, a source of inspiration, and a destination for self-actualization.

2. ***Is your brand the hero?*** People personify the world around them and build relationships with products, services, companies, and countries, not just with other people[19]. Go with it; let your brand become a character in your customers' stories.
3. ***Promise, but deliver!*** As we've seen, brand trust pays off in a big way: in BRAND*cebo* effects for customers and higher profits for companies. Brands must do everything in their power to both *be*, and *be seen as*, trustworthy.
4. ***Your brand—a community organizer:*** To really thrive, a brand must develop an active human-to-human community of support with a shared story, common values, and mutual reinforcement of high expectations.
5. ***Your brand is not what YOU think:*** Remember, while marketers can create messages and experiences, things like brand perception, expectations, and brand trust exist entirely within the minds of your customers. You can hope to shape these things, but the consumers *own* them; respect their property.
6. ***Your customer is your partner:*** Pushing ads at brand-weary audiences is dead. The real business of marketing today is about partnering with your community of consumers to promote the brand they trust, identify with, and feel ownership of. The less people trust advertising, the greater the influence of brand-loyal customers becomes.
7. ***If they love you, they'll work for you:*** Passionate, evangelistic fans drive earned media, our electronic "word of mouth." Your community of loyal consumers will build your brand for you for free, and they will do it more creatively, effectively, and passionately than you could have imagined sitting in your conference room and brainstorming with your team.
8. ***They already talk about you:*** In the all-important digital world,

your company exists today at the speed of light. Your brand, and news about it, can travel faster than ever before. In an eye-blink, consumers see it, search for it, shop for it, and share it. They hold the digital megaphone. You want to empower them to use it to reinforce the positive expectations that will bring in new customers and foment BRAND*cebo* effects.

9. ***They're here. Greet them!*** Through the infinitely cross-connected world of new technology, your access to customers, both new and old, is virtually unlimited. Use it. Stay abreast with the ever-changing landscape of technology and new media as you reach out to new consumers and nurture your community of dependent customers.

ACKNOWLEDGEMENTS

My exciting BRAND*cebo* journey started with the pair of Adidas shoes my parents bought me back in 1973. Back then, I was truly convinced that these shoes made me run faster. Fast-forward 44 years, I suggest in this book that feeling faster with my new shoes was not only in my head. The Adidas BRAND*cebo* actually made me run faster.

So, naturally, I must first thank my parents, Rosette and Albert Malka, for having the foresight to buy me running shoes that would ultimately turn into a book, and then for their dedication (many times at their own expense) to the success and happiness of my brothers, my sister, and I. No words could adequately express my love and admiration for my parents, and I hope that the dedication of this book to them serves as a small token of my eternal gratitude.

Working on BRAND*cebo* over the past couple of years was one of the most captivating, challenging and fulfilling experiences in my life. And, the expression 'it takes a village' was never more real. I could not have done it without the professional and emotional support of some very special people. I would like to thank Karen Lacey for playing a crucial role in putting my thoughts and writings into a coherent manuscript. Karen delved into the research with passion, kept me focused, and confidently guided me through the writing process.

A very special thank you to my great friend and mentor, Melissa Hayden Cook, CEO of Sharp Health Plan, and a marketing strategist extraordinaire, for the constant support and for brilliantly coming up with the term BRAND*cebo* for the book title.

My passion for marketing and branding would have been merely a philosophical exercise without the trust, partnership and support of my clients over the past 20 years. Their respective ingenuity, drive and generous sharing of ideas and knowledge have been an endless source of inspiration to me. I am also truly privileged to be surrounded every day by a team of amazing individuals with incredible talents at Ameba Marketing. In one way or another, every one of them (interns included) contributed to the success of this journey. In particular, I would like to thank my professional right hand, Lauren Avallone, for her intelligent insights and for allowing me the time and space needed to work on the book, and Sarah Schmidt, my extraordinary Art Director for the great cover and jacket design. I would also like to thank Bryna Kranzler for a superb editing job, and Oksana Kravtsova for the beautiful and intelligent book layout and formatting work.

I am sincerely grateful to several people who graciously took the time to read the draft manuscript and offer smart and useful comments and suggestions that greatly improved the outcome. These include Chris Lischewsky, Melissa Hayden Cook, Jean-Marc Bronoel, Michael Elbaz, Claude Benchimol, Tom Carroll, Elke Boegart, Dr. Denis Charbit, Guri Stark, Carine Chitayat, Micha Hershkovitz, and Lauren Avallone.

I would like to thank my amazing kids, Matan, Maya, Sophia and Lior for enduring my sleep-deprived agitation, and for their constant support and encouragement, nonetheless.

And, finally, my dear wife, Ursula Malka. While a lot of people made BRAND*cebo* possible, she was truly my trusted chaperon every step of the way. Her unconditional support, enthusiasm and encouragement were like turbo fuel on a mountainous road. She created and respected the time and space I needed, and was genuinely involved in the progress of each chapter of the book, inspiring me to shoot for nothing short of perfection. If it was even possible, my love and admiration for my wife only grew deeper throughout this experience. I am truly blessed!

NOTES

CHAPTER 1: THE ROAD TO BRAND*cebo*

1 *Like Mike* (2002). On Demand. Story by Michael Elliot; Screenplay by Michael Elliot and Jordan Moffet. Directed by John Schultz. 20th Century Fox.

2 Aaron M. Garvey, Frank Germann, and Lisa E. Bolton. "Performance Brand Placebos: How Brands Improve Performance and Consumers Take the Credit." *J Consum Res* 2016. 42 (6):931-951. https://doi.org/10.1093/jcr/ucv094.

3 Allison, Ralph I., and Kenneth P. Uhl. "Influence of Beer Brand Identification on Taste Perception." *Journal of Marketing Research* 1, no. 3 (1964): 36-39. doi:10.2307/3150054.

4 Ibid.

5 Steve Silberman. "Placebos Are Getting More Effective. Drugmakers Are Desperate to Know Why," *Wired Magazine* 17-09 (08.24.09) http://archive.wired.com/medtech/drugs/magazine/17-09/ff_placebo_effect?currentPage=all.

6 Allison and Uhl. "Influence of Beer Brand Identification on Taste Perception." *Journal of Marketing Research* 1(3) (Aug 1964): 36-39. doi: 10.2307/3150054.

7 Samuel M. McClure, Jian Li, Damon Tomlin, Kim S. Cypert, Latané M. Montague, P. Read Montague. "Neural correlates of behavioral preference for culturally familiar drinks," Neuron 44(2). (Oct 14, 2004): 379-87. doi: 10.1016/j.neuron.2004.09.019.

8 Marcia Purse. "Placebo Definition and Information." *VeryWell.* (July 25, 2016). https://www.verywell.com/what-is-a-plcebo-380359.

9 Ibid.

10 Greg Smith. "Tweens R Shoppers: A Look at the Tween Market & Shopping Behavior." *POPAI: The Global Association for Marketing at Retail.* (March 2013). http://memberconnect.shopassociation.org/HigherLogic/System/DownloadDocumentFile.ashx?DocumentFileKey=e74d8a46-ae5c-c844-9c45-ceb722700418.

11 Pete Forester. "You Won't Believe How Much Nike Spends on 'Demand Creation.'" *Complex* (Jul 26, 2014). http://www.complex.com/sneakers/2014/07/nike-spends-3b-on-demand-creation.

12 Nike, Inc. https://store.nike.com/us/en_us/pw/nike-free-running-shoes/9zmZ8yzZoi3

13 Lucia Moses. "A Look at Kids' Exposure to Ads: Children see a lot of marketing messages, regardless of platform." *AdWeek,* (March 11, 2014):23. http://www.adweek.com/news/advertising-branding/look-kids-exposure-ads-156191.

14 In professional races, only milliseconds separate between gold medal and no medal.

CHAPTER 2: THE KING, THE GOLEM, AND THE RAY-BAN GLASSES

1 Benjamin Phillips, F.R.S. *Scrofula: Its Nature, Its Causes, Its Prevalence, and the Principles of Treatment.* (Philadephia: Lea and Blanchard. 1846):240.

2 "Attributed to the Royal Touch: On the Cure of Scrofulous Disease." *The Archaeological Journal,* volume 10. (1853):204.

3 Henry K. Beecher, MD. "The Powerful Placebo." *JAMA* 159(17) (1955):1602-1606. doi:10.1001/jama.1955.02960340022006.

4 "Fabrizio Benedetti." https://en.wikipedia.org/wiki/Fabrizio_Benedetti

5 Robert Rosenthal and Lenore Jacobson. *Pygmalion in the Classroom.* (New York: Rinehart and Winston Holt, 1968).

6 Rosenthal and Jacobson. "Teachers' expectancies: Determinates of pupils' IQ gains." *Psychological Reports* 19 (1966):115-118.

7 George W. Bush speech to NAACP, July 10, 2000. http://www.washingtonpost.com/wp-srv/onpolitics/elections/bushtext071000.htm.

8 H. Bruce Lipton, *The Biology of Belief.* (CA: Hay House, 2005; revised 2008).

9 Walter B. Cannon. "'VOODOO' Death." *American Anthropologist,* Volume 44. (1942) 169-181. doi: 10.1525/aa.1942.44.2.02a00010.

10 "CentralAustralian Ceremonial Artefacts [sic]—auction results 2004." http://www.duckdigital.net/FOD/FOD1036.html.

11 "Placebo." *The American Heritage Dictionary of the English Language, Fifth Edition.* (Boston:Houghton Mifflin Harcourt Publishing Company. 2017).

12 Rose Eveleth, "Why Do Placebos Work?" *Smithsonian*

Magazine. (December 24, 2012).

[13] Cara Feinchuk, "The Placebo Phenomenon," Harvard Magazine. (January-February 2013). http://harvardmagazine.com/2013/01/the-placebo-phenomenon.

[14] "Nocebo effect." *Merriam-Webster Dictionary.* https://www.merriam-webster.com/dictionary/nocebo.

[15] Joseph Stromberg, "What is the Nocebo Effect?" (July 23, 2012).http://www.smithsonianmag.com/science-nature/what-is-the-nocebo-effect-5451823/.

[16] Moty Amar, Dan Ariely, Maya Bar-Hillel, Ziv Carmon, and Chezy Ofir. "Brand names act like marketing placebos." *The Hebrew University of Jerusalem; Center for the Study of Rationality* (Feb., 2011). http://www.ratio.huji.ac.il/sites/default/files/publications/dp566.pdf.

[17] Ibid.

[18] "Functional magnetic resonance imaging." https://en.wikipedia.org/wiki/Functional_magnetic_resonance_imaging.

[19] McClure, et al. "Neural correlates of behavioral preference for culturally familiar drinks," *Neuron* 44(2) (Oct 14, 2004):379-87. doi: 10.1016/j.neuron.2004.09.019.

[20] Ibid.

[21] Baba Shiv, Ziv Carmon, and Dan Ariely. "Placebo Effects of Marketing Actions: Consumers May Get What They Pay For." *Journal of Marketing Research* 42(4) (November 2005):383-393. doi.org/ 10.1509/jmkr.2005.42.4.383.

CHAPTER 3: ROMANCING THE BRAND

1 Nate Scott. "Study finds that fans of losing NFL teams are more likely to get fat." *USA Today*. (September 4, 2013). http://ftw.usatoday.com/2013/09/study-nfl-fans-losing-teams-fat-obese-fans.

2 Susan Fournier. "Consumers and their brands: Developing relationship theory in consumer research." *Journal of Consumer Research* 24(4) (March 1, 1998):*343-373*. doi: 10.1086/209515.

3 "Southwest Media." https://www.swamedia.com/pages/1972-to-1978.

4 Jannine D. Lasaleta, Constantine Sedikides, and Kathleen D. Vohs. "Nostalgia Weakens the Desire for Money." *Journal of Consumer Research* 41(3) (October 2014):713-729. doi: 10.1086/677227.

5 Seong-Yeon Park and Eun Mi Lee. "Congruence Between Brand Personality and Self-Image, and the Mediating Roles of Satisfaction and Consumer-Brand Relationship on Brand Loyalty." *Asia Pacific Advances in Consumer Research* 6 (2005):39-45.

CHAPTER 4: PRIMING: OF MEN, MICE, AND SODA POP

1 "Johan Cruyff." https://commons.wikimedia.org/wiki/File:Johan-cruyff_la-naranja-mecanica.jpg.

2 "Franz Beckenbauer." https://en.wikipedia.org/wiki/Franz_Beckenbauer.

3 *McClure, et al. "Neural correlates of behavioral preference for culturally familiar drinks," 379-87. doi: 10.1016/j.neuron.2004.09.019.*

4 Illustration from Anatomy & Physiology, Connexions. http://cnx.org/content/col11496/1.6/, accessed June 19, 2013.

5 Robert Ader and Nicholas Cohen. "Behaviorally conditioned immune suppression." *Psychosom Med* 37(4) (Jul-Aug 1975):333-40.

6 Ader and Cohen. "Behaviorally conditioned immune suppression." *Psychosom Med* 333-40.

7 Public Relations Department, University of Rochester Medical Center. "Robert Ader, Founder of Psychoneuroimmunology, Dies." News, University of Rochester Medical Center. (December 20, 2011). https://www.urmc.rochester.edu/news/story/3370/robert-ader-founder-of-psychoneuroimmunology-dies.aspx

8 John A. Bargh, Mark Chen, and Lara Burrows. "Automaticity of social behavior: Direct effects of trait construct and stereotype activation on action." *Journal of Personality and Social Psychology* 71(2) (Aug 1996:230-244.

9 Boundless. "Applications of Classical Conditioning to Human Behavior." *Boundless Psychology* Boundless, 20 Sep. 2016. Retrieved 7 Jul. 2017 from https://www.boundless.com/psychology/textbooks/boundless-psychology-textbook/learning-7/classical-conditioning-46/applications-of-classical-conditioning-to-human-behavior-194-12729/.

10 "Annual per capita consumption of Coca-Cola Company's beverage products from 1991 to 2012, by country (in servings of 8-fluid ounce beverages)." *Statista: The Statistics Portal. https://www.statista.com/statistics/271156/per-capita-consumption-of-soft-drinks-of-the-coca-cola-company-by-country/*

11 *"Global revenue and financial results of the Coca-Cola Company from 2009 to 2016 (in million U.S. dollars)." Statista: The Statistics Portal.* http://www.statista.com/statistics/264423/revenue-and-financial-results-of-coca-cola/.

[12] Kim Bhasin. "15 Facts About Coco-Cola That Will Blow Your Mind." (June 9. 2011). http://www.businessinsider.com/facts-about-coca-cola-2011-6?op=1.

[13] Statistics & Facts on the Coca-Cola Company. https://www.statista.com/topics/1392/coca-cola-company/.

[14] Susan Fournier. "Consumers and their brands: Developing relationship theory in consumer research." *Journal of Consumer Research* 24(4) (March 1, 1998):364. doi: https://doi.org/10.1086/209515.

[15] William M Backer, Roger F. Cook, Roquel Davis, and Roger Greenaway. *I'd Like To Teach The World To Sing.* © Sony/ATV Music Publishing LLC. s

[16] Ibid.

[17] Ibid.

[18] Journal of Economic Behavior & Organization Volume 77, Issue 1, January 2011, Pages 53-65.

[19] Amy Winecoff, John A. Clithero, R. McKell Carter, Sara R. Bergman, Lihong Wang, and Scott A. Huettel. "Ventromedial Prefrontal Cortex Encodes Emotional Value," *Journal of Neuroscience.* 33(27) (Jul 3, 2013):11032–11039. doi: https://doi.org/10.1523/JNEUROSCI.4317-12.201.

[20] From Promotion to Emotion © 2013 The Corporate Executive Board Comp. https://www.cebglobal.com/content/dam/cebglobal/us/EN/best-practices-decision-support/marketing-communications/pdfs/promotion-emotion-whitepaper-full.pdf.

[21] Youchi Kuo, Jeff Walters, Hongbing Gao, Angela Wang, Veronique Yang, Jian Yang, Zhibin Lyu, and Hongjie Wan. "BCG Perspective, The New China Playbook Young, Affluent, E-Savvy Consumers Will Fuel Growth." (December

21, 2015). https://www.bcgperspectives.com/content/articles/globalization-growth-new-china-playbook-young-affluent-e-savvy-consumers/.

[22] JI YI, Meng Fang Yuan, and Suresh Kumah. "The Attitude, motivation influence people's buying Luxury goods: A survey of Chinese in China." *IOSR Journal of Business and Management (IOSR-JBM)* 15(3) (Nov- Dec 2013):15-24 http://iosrjournals.org/iosr-jbm/papers/Vol15-issue3/D01531524.pdf.

[23] Melanie L. Glocker, Daniel D. Langleben, Kosha Ruparel, James W. Loughead, Ruben C. Gur, and Norbert Sachser. "Baby Schema in Infant Faces Induces Cuteness Perception and Motivation for Caretaking in Adults." *Ethology*. 115(3) (Mar 2009): 257–263. doi: 10.1111/j.1439-0310.2008.01603.x.

[24] http://www.neurosciencemarketing.com/blog/articles/baby-pics-boost-altruism.htm/michelin-baby-ad.

[25] "Know Your Brain: Nucleus Accumbens." *Neuroscientifically Challenged* (June 13, 2014). http://www.neuroscientificallychallenged.com/blog/2014/6/11/know-your-brain-nucleus-accumbens.

[26] Glocker, Langleben, Ruparel, Loughead, Gur and Sachser. "Baby Schema in Infant Faces Induces Cuteness Perception and Motivation for Caretaking in Adults." https://www.ncbi.nlm.nih.gov/pmc/articles/PMC3260535/.

[27] H. Holmes. "Coffee Shop Business Overview (SIC Code: 5812 NAICS Code: 72221)." *SBDCNet.* http://www.sbdcnet.org/small-business-research-reports/coffee-shop.

[28] Caglar Irmak. "The placebo effect in marketing: Motivational underpinning." *City University of New York, ProQuest Dissertations* (2007). http://proquest.umi.com/pqdlink?did=1409495511&Fmt=7&clientI d=79356&RQT=309&VName=PQD.

[29] Russell A. Hill and Robert A. Barton. "Psychology: Red enhances human performance in contests," *Nature* 435(293) (May 19, 2005). doi: 10.1038/435293a.

[30] Martin J. Attrill , Karen A. Gresty, Russell A. Hill and Robert A. Barton. "Red shirt colour is associated with long-term team success in English football," *Journal of Sports Sciences* 26(6) (2008):577-582. Doi: doi: 10.1080/02640410701736244.

[31] Daniel Kahneman, D. *Thinking Fast and Slow.* (New York: Farrar, Strauss and Giroux. Farrar, Straus and Giroux, 2013).

[32] Adrian C. North, David J.; Hargreaves and Jennifer McKendrick. "The influence of in-store music on wine selections." *Journal of Applied Psychology* 84(2) (Apr 1999): 271-276. http://dx.doi.org/10.1037/0021-9010.84.2.271.

[33] Adrian C. North. "The effect of background music on the taste of wine," British Journal of Psychology (103)3 (August 2012):293-301.

[34] Gráinne M. Fitzsimmons, Tanya L. Chartrand, Gavan J. Fitzsimmons. "Automatic Effects of Brand Exposure on Motivated Behavior: How Apple Makes You 'Think Different,' *Journal of Consumer Research* 35 (June 2008).

[35] Ibid.

[36] Amos Tversky and Daniel Kahneman. "Judgment under Uncertainty: Heuristics and Biases," *Science* New Series (185)4157 (Sep. 27, 1974):1124-1131.

[37] Ab Litt, Taly Reich, Senia Maymin and Baba Shiv. "Pressure and Perverse Flights to Familiarity," *Psychological Science* 22 (2011):523.

CHAPTER 5: EXPECTATION: BRANDING AND THE ART OF THE SELF-FULFILLING PROPHECY

1 Malcolm Gladwell. *Blink: The Power of Thinking without Thinking.* (New York : Little, Brown and Co., 2005).

2 Timothy A. Judge and Daniel M. Cable. "The Effect of Physical Height on Workplace Success and Income: Preliminary Test of a Theoretical Model," *Journal of Applied Psychology* 89(3) (Jun 2004):428-41.

3 Ibid

4 "Expectation." http://www.merriam-webster.com/dictionary/expectation.

5 Deborah J. MacInnis and Gustavo E. De Mello. "The Concept of Hope and Its Relevance to Product Evaluation and Choice," *Journal of Marketing* 69(1) (January 2005):1-14. https://doi.org/10.1509/jmkg.69.1.1.55513.

6 Stacy Brown. "Considering *Curanderismo*: The Place of Traditional Hispanic Folk Healing in Modern Medicine." *ETHOS*—Boston College Student Bioethics Research Journal 3 (Spring 2008). http://www.bc.edu/clubs/mendel/ethos/archives/2008/brown.shtml.

7 Stanford GSB Staff. "The Behavioral Impact of a Higher Price. " *Insights by Stanford Business.* (March 1, 2008). https://www.gsb.stanford.edu/insights/behavioral-impact-higher-price.

8 Ibid.

9 Vladimir A. Gheorghiu, Peter W. Sheehan and Irving Kirsch.). "Suggestion, suggestibility, and the placebo effect," *Hypnosis International Monographs* 4 (2002):71–90.

10 Connie Peck and Grahame Coleman. ""Implications of placebo theory for clinical research and practice in pain management," Theoretical Medicine and Bioethics 12(3) (Sep 1991):247-70.

[11] Judith A. Turner; Richard A. Deyo, John D. Loeser; et al. "The importance of placebo effects in pain treatment and research," *JAMA.* 271(20).(1994):1609-1614. doi: 10.1001/jama.1994.03510440069036.doi: 10.1001/jama.1994.03510440069036..

[12] Irving Kirsch. "Response expectancy as a determinant of experience and behavior," *American Psychologist* 40, (1985):1189–1202.

[13] Alexander Ploghaus, Irene Tracey, Joseph S. Gati, et al. "Dissociating pain from its anticipation in the human brain," *Science.* (Jun 18, 1999) 284(5422):1979-81. doi: 10.1126/science.284.5422.1979doi: 10.1126/science.284.5422.1979

[14] "Anterior cingulate cortex." Wikipedia: The Free Encyclopedia. https://en.wikipedia.org/wiki/Anterior_cingulate_cortex.

[15] "Insular cortex." Wikipedia: The Free Encyclopedia. https://en.wikipedia.org/wiki/Insular_cortex.

[16] Tor D. Wager, James K. Rilling, Edward E. Smith, Alex Sokolik, Kenneth L. Casey, Richard J. Davidson, Stephen M. Kosslyn, Robert M. Rose, Jonathan D. Cohen. "Placebo-Induced Changes in fMRI in the Anticipation and Experience of Pain." *Science* Vol. 303 no. 5661. (February 2004):1162-1167. http://science.sciencemag.org/content/303/5661/1162.full.

[17] Tor D. Wagner. "The neural bases of placebo effects in pain," *Current Directions in Psychological Science, 14*(4) (Aug 2005): 175-179.

[18] "Emaze: Amazing Presentations." https://www.emaze.com/@AIWFOOFT/Presentation-Name.

[19] Alia J. Crum and Ellen J. Langer.. Mind-set matters: Exercise and the placebo effect, *Psychological Science, 18*(2) (2007): 165-171. doi: 10.1111/j.1467-9280.2007.01867.xdoi: 10.1111/j.1467-9280.2007.01867.x.

[20] Ellen L. Idler and Stanislav Kasl. "Health perception and survival: Do global evaluations of health status predict mortality?" *Journals of Gerontology* 46(2) (1991):S55-S65. https://doi.org/10.1093/geronj/46.2.S55.

[21] George A. Kaplan and Terry Camacho. (1983). Perceived health and mortality: A nine-year follow-up of the human population laboratory cohort. *American Journal of Epidemiology 177* (April 1993):292–304. doi: 10.1093/oxfordjournals.aje.a113541doi: 10.1093/oxfordjournals.aje.a113541.

[22] Robert Buckman and Karl Sabbagh. *Magic or Medicine: An Investigation of Healing and Healers.* (London:: Macmillan, 1993).

[23] "Developmental Skills increased with Baby Einstein." *Baby Einstein Testimonial Materials.* http://commercialfreechildhood.org/sites/default/files/Attachment%204%20-%20BE%20testimonial%20headings.pdf

[24] Ibid

[25] Ibid.

[26] http://www.teslarati.com/brilliant-tesla-advertising-strategy-lack-thereof/.

[27] Dylan Love. "Netflix recommendation engine drives 75% of viewership." *Business Insider.* (April 9, 2012). http://www.businessinsider.com/netflixs-recommendation-engine-drives-75-of-viewership-2012-4.

[28] "Local Consumer Review Survey: 2016. "https://www.brightlocal.com/learn/local-consumer-review-survey/.

[29] Amy Gensenhues. "Survey: 90% Of Customers Say Buying Decisions Are Influenced By Online Reviews." *Marketing Land.* (April 9, 2013). http://marketingland.com/survey-customers-more-frustrated-by-how-long-it-takes-to-resolve-a-customer-service-issue-than-the-resolution-38756.

CHAPTER 6: DESIRE: MIRROR, MIRROR ON THE WALL

1 Sandra Forsythe, Mary Frances Drake and Charles E. Cox. "Influence of Applicant's Dress on Interviewer's Selection Decisions," *Journal of Applied Psychology* 70(2)(1985):374.

2 Arthur Aron, Christian Norman and Elaine Nancy Aron. "The self-expansion model and motivation," *Representative Research in Social Psychology* 22 (1998):1–13.

3 Anne Harrington. *The placebo effect: An interdisciplinary phenomenon.* (Cambridge: Harvard University Press, 1999).

4 Caglar Irmak, Lauren G. Block, and Gavan J. Fitzsimons. "The placebo effect in marketing: Sometimes you just have to want it to work," *Journal of Marketing Research (42) (2005):*406–409; Moty Amar, Dan Ariely, Maya Bar-Hillel, et. al. "*Brand names act like marketing placebos.*" Retrieved from http://www.ratio.huji.ac.il/dp_files/dp566.pdf.

5 Ibid.

6 Rebecca Erwin Wells. "To Tell the Truth, the Whole Truth, May Do Patients Harm: The Problem of the Placebo Effect for Informed Consent." *Am J Bioeth* 12(3) (Mar 2012):22–29. doi: 10.1080/15265161.2011.652798.

7 (Ibid.

8 A.J. Douglas. "*Central noradrenergic mechanisms underlying acute stress responses of the Hypothalamo–pituitary–adrenal axis: adaptations through pregnancy and lactation,*" *Stress 8*(1) (March 2005):5–18.

9 David Robson. "The contagious thought that could kill you." *BBC.* (February 11, 2015). http://www.bbc.com/future/story/20150210-can-you-think-yourself-to-death.

10 Doron Malka, Ameba Marketing.

CHAPTER 7: THE RICOCHET EFFECT

1 Mary A. Burke and Tim R. Sass. "Classroom peer effects and student achievement," *National Center for Analysis of Longitudinal Data in Educational Research, Journal of Labor Economics* (31)1 (January 2013):51-82.

2 Jason Fletcher. "Spillover effects of inclusion of classmates with emotional problems on test scores in early elementary school," *Journal of Policy Analysis and Management* 29(1) (September 2010):69-83.

3 Todd D. Kendall, T.. Spillovers, complementarities, and sorting in labor markets with an application to professional sports. *Southern Economic Journal, 70*(2) (2003):389 402.

4 Ibid.

5 Eric D. Gould and Eyal Winter. "Interactions between workers and the technology of production: Evidence from professional baseball," *The Review of Economics and Statistics 91*(1) (February 2009):188-200.

6 Kerry L. Papps. "*The dynamics of productivity spillovers in Major League Baseball," Doctoral dissertation, Cornell University* (2008). https://editorialexpress.com/cgi-bin/conference/download.cgi?db_name=res2008&paper_id=769.

7 John C. Bradbury and Douglas J. Drinen. "Pigou at the Plate: Externalities in Major League Baseball," *Journal of Sports Economics* 9(2) (2008):211-224.

8 Ibid.

9 Gabriel Rossman, Nicole Esparza, Phillip Bonacich. "I'd like to thank the academy, team spillovers, and network centrality," *American Sociological Review 75*(1) (2010):31-51.

10 Ibid.

[11] Seth Freedman, Melissa Kearney and Mara Lederman. "How Did Consumers Respond to the Toy Recalls of 2007?" Economics, University of California at Irvine (2009). http://www.economics.uci.edu/files/docs/micro/s09/kearney.pdf.

[12] Laurie A. Rudman and Eugene Borgida. "The afterglow of construct accessibility: the behavioral consequences of priming men to view women as sexual objects," *Journal of Experimental Social Psychology* 31(6)(1995):493–517.

[13] Alexandre Mas and Enrico Moretti. "Peers at work," *American Economic Review* 99(1)(2009):112-145.

[14] R.A. Rescorla and Allan R. Wagner. (1972). "A theory of Pavlovian conditioning: Variations in the effectiveness of reinforcement and nonreinforcement," In *Classical Conditioning II: Current theory and research,* eds. Abraham H. Black and William Frederick Prokasy. (New York :Appleton-Century-Crofts, 1972):64–99.

CHAPTER 8: BUILDING BRAND*cebo*

[1] Doron Malka, Ameba Marketing.

[2] Saatchi & Saatchi, *Red Paper: Brand Loyalty Reloaded 2015.* http://www.saatchikevin.com/wp-content/uploads/2014/09/Loyalty-Beyond-Reason-Red-Paper-Jan-2015.pdf.

[3] Ibid.

[4] Ibid.

[5] Ibid.

[6] Gensler.com. *"Is emotional connection the key to customer engagement?"* 2013 Brand Engagement Survey: The Emotional Power of Brands. https://www.gensler.com/research-insight/research/2013-brand-engagement-survey.

[7] Ibid.

8 Doron Malka, Ameba Marketing.

9 Daniel E. Moerma. *Meaning, Medicine and the 'Placebo Effect'* in Cambridge Studies in Medical Anthropology (Book 9). (Cambridge: Cambridge University Press, 2002).

10 Doron Malka, Ameba Marketing.

11 Amy Gallo. "*The Value of Keeping the Right Customers,*" Harvard Business Review (October 29, 2014). https://hbr.org/2014/10/the-value-of-keeping-the-right-customers.

12 Ibid.

13 Ibid.

14 Saatchi & Saatchi, *Red Paper: Brand Loyalty Reloaded 2015.*

15 Ibid.

16 Holmes. "Coffee Shop Business Overview."

17 Rachel Tepper. "*Starbucks Brand Loyalty Keeps It Ahead Of The Artisanal Coffee Movement,*" HuffPost. (March 7, 2013). http://www.huffingtonpost.com/2013/03/07/starbucks-brand-loyalty_n_2830372.html.

18 Ray Oldenburg. *The Great Good Place: Cafes, Coffee Shops, Bookstores, Bars, Hair Salons, and Other Hangouts at the Heart of a Community. (New York: Marlowe & Company, 1999).*

19 Susan Fournier, "Consumers and their brands: Developing relationship theory in consumer research." *Journal of Consumer Research* 24(4)(March 1, 1998):*343-373.* doi: 10.1086/209515.

INDEX

APPENDIX A:
The Placebo Effect Of Brands Research Methodology

INTRODUCTION

Studies of the placebo effect in marketing focused, thus far, on the effect resulting from a change or manipulation of one marketing element—primarily price—and condition, expectancy and motivation as main drivers producing the placebo effect with adults (Shiv et al., 2005b; Berns, 2005; Irmak, 2007). While this study was built upon those principles, it particularly focused on brand recognition and perception as triggers of the placebo effect, practically following foundational research conducted by Makens (1964), Allison and Uhl (1964), and later, Amar et al. (2011). This study, therefore, focused on the extent to which children's recognition of a particular brand of running shoes and their positive perceptions of that brand affected their performance in a 50-meter run.

Hypothesis 1(a) is for RQ1, and formally states that:

Hypothesis 1(a): Participants who are exposed to the superior attributes of the brand, and use it in the experiment, will experience a placebo effect, positively affecting their performance in a 50-meter run.

Hypothesis 1(b) is for RQ2, and formally states that:

Hypothesis 1(b): Participants who are exposed to the superior attributes of the brand, but do not use it in the experiment, will experience a spillover effect, negatively affecting their performance in a 50-meter run.

To test theses hypotheses, Test 1 was divided into two parts. In Part I, all participants ran with the "knockoff" shoe (disguised brand), and following a conditioning intervention (valued brand introduction) in Part II, 50% of the participants ran with the valued brand, while the other 50% continued to run with the "knockoff" shoe. Data from Test1, Part I were compared with data from Test 1, Part II.

Independent Variables: Type of shoe ("knockoff" vs. "real": categorical).

Dependent Variable: Time recorded in a 50-meter run (continuous)

Building upon the classical conditioning, expectancy and motivational theories established by Shiv et al. (2005), Berns, (2005), and Irmak, (2007), this study further suggested that 1) following an introduction to the superior attributes of a brand, there would be a significant difference in expectation and motivation levels between participants who can use the brand and those who were exposed to it but cannot use it; and 2) expectation and motivation directly affect performance. Hypotheses 2(a) and 2(b) are for RQ1 and RQ2:

Hypothesis 2(a): Exposing participants to a brand's superior attributes will result in a statistically significant difference in the motivation and performance expectation levels between participants who are able to use the brand and those who were exposed to the brand's superior attributes, but cannot use it.

Hypothesis 2(b): There is a statistically significant correlation between motivation and performance expectation scores and the performance difference in running time of participant in both Placebo and Spillover groups.

Independent Variables: Type of shoe ("knockoff" vs. "real": categorical).

Dependent Variable: 1) Brand expectation (ordinal); 2) Brand motivation (ordinal).

Additionally, this study assumed that time must be considered as an important factor in sustaining the strength of the placebo effect and the spillover effect. Hypothesis 3 is for RQ3 and formally states that:

Hypothesis 3: The placebo effect and spillover effect generated by positive perception of the brand will diminish over time, and children's performance in a 50-meter run will be closer to baseline levels.

Independent Variable: Type of shoe ("knockoff" vs. "real": categorical).

Dependent Variable: Time recorded in a 50-meter run (continuous).

To test this hypothesis, participants' running times in Test 2 were compared with their running times at Baseline.

Two quasi-experimental (due to the non-random nature of the sample) studies were conducted to effectively test the hypotheses specified above. The first experiment tested both hypotheses 1a and 1b, and demonstrated whether the placebo effect and spillover effect were created by brand recognition and perception. The second experiment was conducted seven days after the first study, and tested hypothesis 3, specifically investigating whether performance levels affected by placebo and spillover in the first study still held over time.

SELECTION OF PARTICIPANTS

This study used a convenience sampling of school children participating in physical education (PE) classes. To ensure statistical reliability, the sample consisted of 100 boys and 100 girls, 9 to 13 years old, attending school in San Diego County. As part of their normal class schedule, students attended PE classes on a daily basis. The sample for this study consisted of students in two PE classes in two different schools. Twenty-three students did not complete all required elements of the experiment and, therefore, were eliminated from the study, leaving a total of 177 qualified participants for whom data analysis was performed.

This cohort is the fringe of what is referred to in the demographic literature as "tweens," children in the transition between being adolescent to becoming a teenager (LaChance, Beaudoin, & Robitaille, 2003). According to Smith (2013), this demographic cohort in the U.S. consists of over 20 million boys and girls and is, directly and indirectly, responsible for about $200 billion of spending per year (see Figure 3). Tweens' straightforward, well-informed and well-defined sense of style is critical to the success of current brands and the effective emergence of future brands. This might explain the fact that marketers spend an estimated $17 billion annually to grab their attention and support (Smith, 2013).

Tweens are extremely brand conscious, and use brands to establish social status and acceptance. According to Smith (2013);

Tweens are the most brand-conscious generation yet and are exposed to over 30,000 brands. With such prevalence, it is no wonder that for tweens it is far more important to wear the right label than it is to wear the right clothes. (p. 6)

The right label, according to Achenreiner (2003), means the right brand name.

Achenreiner (2003) conducted a study with children 8, 12, and 16 years old in an attempt to determine at which age in that range brand names alone play a significant factor in their perceptual judgment. Participants were asked to evaluate two advertisements for an athletic shoe. The shoes were physically identical, however one boasted the highly respected brand name Nike®, while the other was presented under the lower regarded brand name Kmart®. The study results indicated that participants predominantly judged the Nike® shoe a better quality, much "cooler" shoe than the Kmart® shoe, not realizing they were evaluating the exact same shoe. These results were most prominent among the 12-year old participants (Achenreiner, 2003).

INSTRUMENTATION

This quantitative study used two types of measurement instruments:

1. Two separate Likert-type surveys (see Appendices A and B) to measure independent variables:
    a. Participants' expectations, following a conditioning intervention, with regard to brand efficacy and their performance with the brand
    b. Participants' motivation, following a conditioning intervention, to experience improved performance
2. A summary sheet including student number and running time in each test (see Appendices C, D, and E). A stopwatch was used to measure running time in a 50-meter run measured over four different instances: 1) participants run with their own shoes; 2) participants run with branded shoes (Nike®) disguised as knockoffs;

3) half of participants run with branded shoes (Nike®), and half run with branded shoes (Nike®) disguised as knockoffs; 4) fourteen days later, participants run with their own shoes.

INSTRUMENT 1: SURVEY

To test the assumptions indicated in hypotheses 1 and 2, participants experienced a conditioning intervention, which included reading and viewing information regarding the brand of running shoes that was utilized in the experiment. Following the conditioning intervention, and prior to conducting test number 2 (half of participants run with branded shoes, and half run with branded shoes disguised as knockoffs), all participants were handed two different survey questionnaires.

The first survey measured participants' overall expectation of brand and personal performance, and included the following questions:

1. How likely is it that the Nike® Free Run 5.0 shoes you just learned about will deliver the performance it promised to?
2. How likely is it that the Nike® Free Run 5.0 shoes you just learned about will improve your running-speed if you were to wear it in the race?

Participants answered these questions using a five-point Likert scale in which "1" would indicate "not likely at all" and "5" would indicate "very likely."

The second survey measured participants' overall motivation to experience the brand's promised attributes, and to improve personal performance, and included the following questions:

1. How much would you like this pair of Nike® Free Run 5.0 shoes to improve your running speed?
2. How much would you like this pair of Nike® Free Run 5.0 shoes to help you win the race?

Participants answered these questions using a five-point Likert scale in which "1" would indicate "not at all" and "5" would indicate "very much."

INSTRUMENT 2: RUNNING TIME SUMMARY SHEET

A summary sheet including student number and running time in each test (see Appendices C, D, and E) was utilized to record participants' performance. An Ultrak 499 professional stopwatch was utilized to measure and record participants' running times in the 50-meter run (dependent variable in all hypotheses).

METHODOLOGICAL ASSUMPTIONS

As in all social and behavioral research, this study also stood the test of validity and relabiity. Whilethese issues are, by and large, mitigated in a quantitative research method, which isolates investigated categories, other tools were utilized to ensure that this reaearch ultimately investigated what it set to investigate and could be replicated under similar conditionins.

The normal distribution of the pre-test results was evaluated to ensure that no skipped questions or errors due to misunderstanding of questions or specific words occurred, and that questions in the survey were clear and easy to understand. Using SPSS software version 21 for statistical analysis, a Cronbach alpha statistical test was conducted in order to ensure that results adhered to the study's objective of 95% co-efficient interval (or α = .05%) and represented a high level of statistical significance. This also ensured reliability and applicability of the results to the general participant's population.

PROCEDURE

One hundred seventy seven students (*N*= 177: 85 boys and 92 girls) attending two San Diego schools participated in this study. Following approval by the school administration and study coordination with the appropriate Physical Education teachers, participation consent letters were sent to parents, and an additional participation consent letter was signed by every student participating in the study.

Two different schools, and two classes from each school, participated in the study. Students ran in pairs, or four at a time, during a normal PE class. Students' shoe sizes were collected in advance. A total of 40 pairs of Nike® Free Run 5.0 shoes (see Figure 4) were used in the study. Twenty pairs used disguised brand name and symbols, and 20 pairs with visible brand name and symbols. A shoe disinfectant spray was used as participants shared the shoes throughout the experiment.

Figure 4. Nike® Free Run 5.0

Four data measurements were collected during the study. The first measurement consisted of participants' running time in the 50-meter run at a baseline level in their own shoes. This data was measured on the running track, using a stopwatch and recorded in a Running Time Summary Sheet (see Appendices C, D, and E). The second measurement, Test 1, Part I, was collected 15-minutes after the baseline measurement, with all participants running with "knockoff" shoes (shoes with completely disguised brand elements). This data was subsequently measured utilizing the same instrument as in the previous run.

The third measurement was collected following a conditioning treatment, which was conducted at the track. Expectancy questionnaires (see Appendix A), and Motivational questionnaires (see Appendix B) were distributed to all participants after the conditioning treatment, and before they conducted Test 1, Part II (half of participants ran with branded shoes, specifically Nike®, and half ran with branded shoes, Nike®, disguised as knockoffs). This was the only time the questionnaires were used. The fourth set of data was collected seven days after the initial intervention, with participants running with their own shoes. The running times were recorded utilizing the same instrument at each stage of data collection.

In summary, the research design consisted of a quasi-experimental, multi-stage design with four repeated measurements; 1) baseline, 2) pre-placebo, 3) placebo + spillover, and 4) longitudinal placebo with an intervention in Test 1 between Part I and Part II

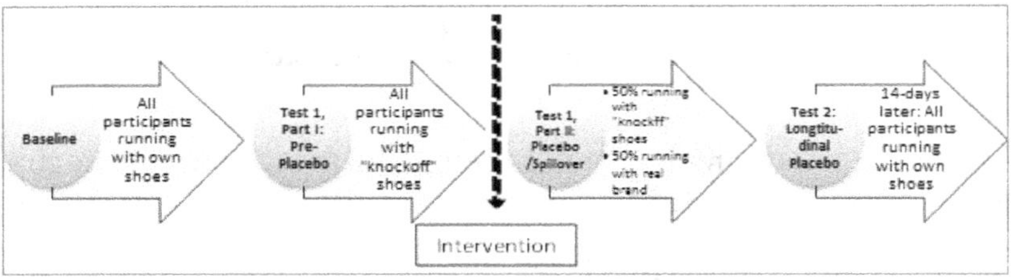

Figure 5. Research Procedure

DATA PROCESSING AND ANALYSIS

Using the SPSS software for statistical analysis, a Cronbach alpha statistic test was conducted in order to ensure results adhered to the study's objective of 95% co-efficient interval (or $\alpha = .05\%$) and represented a high level of statistical significance. This also ensured reliability and applicability of the results to the general participant's population.

Following basic frequency analysis, paired sample t-tests were conducted to test the four hypotheses in Test 1 (Parts I and II), evaluating the placebo effect in run-time performance among participants who were using shoes considered as "branded" (Placebo group) versus those who were using shoes considered as "knockoff" (Spillover group).

The paired samples *t*-test methodology has been successfully utilized in experimental and non-experimental settings to determine whether there are significant differences between matched measurements of results repeated under diverse conditions. It has been utilized in the social sciences to evaluate the strength of intervention responses (Chapman et al., 2009) in the cognitive-behavioral sciences to evaluate treatment effectiveness for mental health outcomes (Frazier et al., 2004), and in the educational sciences to evaluate the effect of knowledge on attitudinal outcomes (Bradley, Waliczek, & Zajicek, 1999). Thus, it was deemed an appropriate approach to evaluate data in this study.

Additionally, the Mann-Whitney Wilcoxon (MWU) test was utilized to compare the expectation and motivation scores of the placebo against the non-placebo group. The MWU test is a non-parametric tool utilized to measure the central tendency of one population against another, and has been successfully utilized in the measurement of Likert-type scale responses (De Winter & Dodou, 2010). In order to establish whether participants' expressed expectation and motivation affected their actual performance (hypothesis 2[a]), a Pearson Correlation analysis was conducted.

Finally, a paired samples *t*-test was used again to compare participants' mean performance in Test 1, Part II (following the placebo and spillover effects) and their Baseline performance, in order to determine whether there a longitudinal impact is generated by the placebo effect or the spillover effect. The following chapter summarizes the findings of all the experimental tests.

RESEARCH RESULTS

OVERVIEW

The purpose of this study was to demonstrate that positive brand perception can directly impact performance, of not only the person using the brand, but also, through a spillover effect, the performance of a person who is exposed to the brand, but is unable to use it.

Two hundred children ages 9 to 13 years old participated in this study. Twenty-three students did not complete all required elements of the experiment and, therefore, were eliminated from the study, leaving a total of 177 (N=177) qualified participants for whom data analysis was performed.

VARIABLES IN THE STUDY

The independent variable, type of shoe, included two levels: (a) "branded" and (b) "knockoff". The dependent variables included continuous variables consisting of repeated measures of running time under different conditions, and four categorical variables measuring participants' expectation and motivation with regards to their performance.

Table 1.

Gender Distribution

		f	%
	Male	85	48.0
Valid	Female	92	52.0
	Total	177	100.0

RESULTS

Sample characteristics

Data was entered into SPSS version 21 for analysis. The initial descriptive exploration revealed the characteristics as shown in Table 1 and 2.

Table 2.

Average Running Scores (Baseline, Tests 1,2 &3)

	Min	Max	*M*	*SD*
Running score with own shoes	6.03	11.84	8.5797	.87445
Test 1—Pre-Placebo (all with nonbranded)	6.16	11.77	8.5032	.86443
Test 2—Placebo + Spillover (50% branded; 50% nonbranded)	6.18	10.89	8.4079	.88168
Test 3—Longitudinal Placebo (all with own shoes)	6.15	11.52	8.6196	.82889

Testing was performed under the assumption of a normally distributed sample with a mean μ and standard deviation σ.

Test 1: The Placebo and Spillover Effects

The purpose of Test 1 was to determine whether recognition of a running shoe brand impacts participants' performance in a 50-meter run. The test was divided into two parts. In Part I, all participants were asked to run in shoes with no brand identification ("Knockoff"). In Part II, the branded shoe was introduced to all participants (conditioning intervention). Half of the participants were asked to run with the branded shoes, while the other half were asked to run again with the "knockoff" shoe.

Hypothesis 1(a): Participants who are exposed to the superior attributes of the brand, and use it in the experiment, will experience a placebo effect, positively affecting their performance in a 50-meter run.

Hypothesis 1(b): Participants who are exposed to the superior attributes of the brand, but do not use it in the experiment, will experience a spillover effect, negatively affecting their performance in a 50-meter run.

Two paired samples *t*-test were utilized to evaluate Hypotheses 1(a) and 1(b). Consistent with this study's hypothesis, there was a significant increase in running time between the pre-placebo Test 1, Part I (all participants running with disguised "knockoff" shoes), and Test 1, Part II, participants running in the placebo and spillover groups (50% running with visible brand; 50% running with disguised "knockoff" brand).

Tables 3, 4, 5, and 6 illustrate the findings for Test 1:

Placebo Group: Branded "Real" Shoes

Table 3.

Paired Samples Statistics—Placebo Group

Pair 1	*M*	*N*	*SD*	*SEM*
Test 1, Part I—Pre-Placebo (all with nonbranded)	8.51	93	.87	.08975
Test 1, Part II—Placebo + Spillover (50% branded; 50% nonbranded)	8.09	93	.80	.08324

The findings in Table 3 and Table 4 indicated a significant decrease in running time for participants running with the branded ("real") shoes (see hypothesis 1a above). From M= 8.51 seconds, SD = .87 seconds to M=8.09 seconds SD =. 80 seconds, at the .00 level of significance, t=-12.38, df=92, n= 93, p < .00, 95% CI for mean difference .35 to .48, r =.93. Hence, these finding reject the null hypothesis and support the alternative hypothesis (H1a), which states: "Participants who are exposed to the superior attributes of the brand, and use it in the experiment, will experience a placebo effect, positively affecting their performance in a 50-meter run."

Table 4.

Paired Samples Test—Placebo Group

				95% CI				
	M	*SD*	*SEM*	Lower	Upper	*t*	*df*	Sig. (2-tailed)
Test 1, Part I—Pre-Placebo (all with nonbranded)—Test 1, Part II—Placebo + Spillover (50% branded; 50% nonbranded)	.417	.325	.03368	.35	.48	12.38	92	.000

Note. CI= Confidence Interval

Spillover Group: "Knockoff" Shoes

Conversely, for participants running with the "knockoff" shoes (the spillover group—see H1b above), there was a significant increase in running time. From *M*= 8.49 seconds, *SD* = .87 seconds to *M*=8.76 seconds *SD* =84 seconds, at the .00 level of significance, *t*=-5.54, *df*=83, *n*= 84, $p < .00$, 95% CI for mean difference -.35 to -.17, *r* =.87. Hence, these findings reject the null hypothesis and support the alternative (H1b) hypothesis, which states: "Participants who are exposed to the superior attributes of the brand, but do not use it in the experiment, will experience a spillover effect, negatively affecting their performance in a 50-meter run."

Table 5.
Paired Samples Statistics—Spillover Group ("Knockoff")

		M	*N*	*SD*	*SEM*
Pair 1	Test 1, Part I—Pre-Placebo (all with nonbranded)	8.49	84	.86835	.09474
	Test 1, Part II—Placebo + Spillover (50% branded; 50% nonbranded)	8.76	84	.83591	.09121

Research findings are congruent with this study's proposed hypotheses 1(a) and 1(b), and confirm that there is a statistically significant difference in the mean running time between the "placebo" and "spillover" groups and a statistically significant difference in the mean running time in Test 1, Part I versus Test 1, Part II, within each group of participants, namely: the "placebo" group ran faster, on average, in Test 1, Part II, while the "spillover" group ran slower, on average, in Test 1, Part II. Both hypotheses 1(a) and 1(b) were, therefore, confirmed.

Hypothesis 2(a): Exposing participants to a brand's superior attributes will result in a statistically significant difference in the motivation and performance expectation levels between participants who are able to use the brand and those who were exposed to the brand's superior attributes, but cannot use it.

Table 6.
Paired Samples Test- Spillover Group

				95% CI				
	M	*SD*	*SEM*	Lower	Upper	*t*	*df*	Sig. (2-tailed)
Test 1, Part I—Pre-Placebo (all with nonbranded)—Test 1, Part II—Placebo + Spillover (50% branded; 50% nonbranded)	-.26	.43	.047	-.35	-.17	-5.5	83	.000

Note. CI= Confidence Interval

Four Mann-Whitney ranks comparison tests were utilized to evaluate Hypothesis 2(a), namely, that there is a significant difference in the motivation and performance expectation scores of children running with "real" branded shoes vs. those running with "knockoff" non-branded shoes (see Appendices A and B). The two scores for expectation and the two scores for motivation were compared between the Placebo group (participants using branded "real" shoes) versus the Spillover group (participants using non-banded "knockoff" shoes). Consistent with this study's hypothesis, there was a significant difference in one out of the two expectation scores and both of the motivation scores between test and non-placebo groups.

Table 7.

Ranks

	Brand	*N*	*MR*	*SR*
Expectation 1—Expectation of branded shoe to deliver on performance promises	Branded	93	89.13	8289.00
	Disguised	84	88.86	7464.00
Expectation 2—Expectation of branded/ nonbranded shoe to improve running speed	Branded	93	124.78	11605.00
	Disguised	84	49.38	4148.00
Motivation 1—Motivation to improve running speed	Branded	93	111.07	10329.50
	Disguised	84	64.57	5423.50
Motivation 2—Motivation to have branded/ nonbranded shoes to help win race	Branded	93	115.46	10737.50
	Disguised	84	59.71	5015.50

Note. Total *N* for each category =177, *MI*=Mean Rank, *SR*= Sum of Ranks

The results of the Mann Whitney U Test, comparing the median scores for expectation 1 ("How likely is it that the Nike® Free Run 5.0 shoes you just learned about will deliver the performance it promised to?") between the non-placebo group wearing "knockoff" shoes and the placebo group wearing "real" shoes, found that these scores were not significantly different between the two groups (z=-.038, $p < .001$).

Conversely, scores for expectation 2 ("How likely is it that the Nike® Free Run 5.0 shoes you just learned about will improve your running-speed?") were found to be significantly different between the two groups (z=-10.08, $p < .001$). The mean score for the group using non-branded shoes was 49.4 whereas the mean rank for the group running with branded shoes was higher at 124.8.

Table 8.
Test Statistics [a]

	E1	E2	M1	M2
Mann-Whitney U	3894.000	578.000	1853.500	1445.500
Wilcoxon W	7464.000	4148.000	5423.500	5015.500
z	-.038	-10.081	-6.242	-7.460
Asymp. Sig. (2-tailed)	.970	.000	.000	.000

Note. ***a*** Grouping Variable: Brand/Non Brand. E1 = Expectation of branded shoe to deliver on performance promises; E2 = Expectation of branded/nonbranded shoe to improve running speed; M1 = Motivation to improve running speed; M2 = Motivation to have branded/nonbranded shoes to help win race.

Scores for motivation 1 ("How much would you like this pair of Nike® Free Run 5.0 shoes to improve your running speed?") were found to be significantly different between the two groups (z=-6.24, $p < .001$). The mean score for the group using non-branded shoes was 64.57 whereas the mean rank for the group running with branded shoes was higher at 111.07. The mean score for the group using non-branded shoes was 49.4 whereas the mean rank for the group running with branded shoes was higher at 124.8.

Scores for motivation 2 ("How much would you like this pair of Nike® Free Run 5.0 shoes to help you win the race?") were found to be significantly different between the two groups (z=-7.46, $p <$ .001). The mean score for the group using non-branded shoes was 59.71 whereas the mean rank for the group running with branded shoes was higher at 115.46.

The findings above are congruent with this study's proposed hypothesis 2(a), namely, that there is a significant difference in the motivation and performance expectation scores of children running with "real" branded shoes vs. those running with "knockoff" non-branded shoes.

Hypothesis 2 (b): There is a statistically significant correlation between motivation and performance expectation scores and the performance difference in running time of participant in both Placebo and Spillover groups.

Table 9.
Correlations

		E1	E2	M1	M2	diff
E1	Pearson Correlation	1	.093	.110	.116	.053
	Sig. (2-tailed)		.219	.146	.124	.487
	N	177	177	177	177	177
E2	Pearson Correlation	.093	1	.472**	.495**	.475**
	Sig. (2-tailed)	.219		.000	.000	.000
	N	177	177	177	177	177
M1	Pearson Correlation	.110	.472**	1	.499**	.357**
	Sig. (2-tailed)	.146	.000		.000	.000
	N	177	177	177	177	177
M2	Pearson Correlation	.116	.495**	.499**	1	400**
	Sig. (2-tailed)	.124	.000	.000		.000
	N	177	177	177	177	177
diff	Pearson Correlation	.053	.475**	.357**	.400**	1
	Sig. (2-tailed)	.487	.000	.000	.000	
	N	177	177	177	177	177

Note. ** Correlation is significant at the 0.01 level (2-tailed). E1 = Expectation of branded shoe to deliver on performance promises; E2 = Expectation of branded/nonbranded shoe to improve running speed; M1 = Motivation to improve running speed; M2 = Motivation to have branded/nonbranded shoes to help win race.

Correlation analysis was performed to test hypothesis 2(b), namely, that there is a statistically significant correlation between motivation and performance expectation scores and the performance difference in running time of participant in both placebo and non-placebo groups. A preliminary step in the correlation analysis was to subtract the running time for Test 2 from the running time scores for Test 1. The difference of these scores was recorded as a continuous measure of performance change across both groups. Subsequently, the newly created performance change score was correlated with the two expectation scores and the two motivation scores. Table 9 illustrates the findings.

The correlation analysis showed that there was a significant positive correlation between the difference score for running time of participants and the score for Expectation 2 ("How likely is it that the Nike® Free Run 5.0 shoes you just learned about will improve your running-speed?"), Motivation 1 ("How much would you like this pair of Nike® Free Run 5.0 shoes to improve your running speed?"), and Motivation 2 ("How much would you like this pair of Nike® Free Run 5.0 shoes to help you win the race?"). These findings further support Hypothesis 2(b) and confirm that participants' expectation and motivation levels strongly correlate with their running performance.

TEST 2: LONGITUDINAL PLACEBO AND SPILLOVER EFFECT

Hypothesis 3: The placebo effect and spillover effect generated by positive perception of the brand will diminish over time, and children's performance in a 50-meter run will be closer to baseline levels.

Table 10.

Paired Samples Statistics—All Participants

		M	*N*	*SD*	*SEM*
Pair 1	Baseline: Running score with own shoes	8.5797	177	.87445	.06573
	Test 2: Longitudinal Placebo (all with own shoes)	8.6196	177	.82889	.06230

Two paired samples t-tests were utilized to evaluate Hypothesis 3, namely, that the placebo effect and spillover effect would diminish overtime and return to baseline levels. Table 10 illustrates the findings for test 2:

Table 11.

Paired Samples Test—All Participants

				95% CI				
	M	*SD*	*SEM*	Lower	Upper	*t*	*df*	Sig. (2-tailed)
Baseline: Running score with own shoes Test 2: Longitudinal Placebo (all with own shoes)	-.03994	.41566	.03124	-.10160	.02172	-1.278	176	.203

Note. CI= Confidence Interval

Consistent with this study's hypothesis, there was no significant difference between participants' running times in Test 2 and their running time at Baseline (*M*= 8.58 seconds, *SD* = .78 seconds at Baseline and *M*=8.62 seconds. *SD* = .81 seconds in Test 2), *t*=-1.28, *df*=176, *p* > .05.

Investigating further within the two groups of participants, namely the "Placebo" group and the "spillover" group, revealed interesting results. The findings showed that no statistically significant difference was found in the running scores in Test 2 versus Baseline for the "placebo" group: *M*=8.53 seconds, *SD*=.87 seconds at Baseline, and *M*=8.57 seconds, *SD*=.93 seconds in Test 2), *t*=-1.14, *df*=92, *p* > .05. (See Tables 12 and 13).

Table 12.

Paired Samples Statistics—Placebo Group

		M	*N*	*SD*	*SEM*
Pair 1	Test 2—Longitudinal Placebo—"Placebo" Group (all with own shoes)	8.5308	93	.86843	.09005
	Running score with own shoes (Placebo Group)	8.5745	93	.93180	.09662

Table 13.

Paired Samples Test—Placebo Group

				95% CI				
	M	*SD*	*SEM*	Lower	Upper	*t*	*df*	Sig. (2-tailed)
Test 2—Longitudinal Placebo—"Placebo" Group (all with own shoes)—Running score with own shoes (Placebo Group)	-.04376	.37	.038	-.12010	.03258	-1.139	92	.258

Note. CI= Confidence Interval

Conversely, a significant difference was revealed between Test 2 and Baseline running times for the "Spillover" group: from *M*= 8.72 seconds, *SD*= .78 seconds, to *M*=8.59 seconds, *SD* =. 81 seconds, *t*=-2,74, *df*=83, *n*=84, *p* < .00 (see Tables 14 and 15).

Table 14.
Paired Samples Statistics—Spillover Group

		M	*N*	*SD*	*SEM*
Pair 1	Test 2—Longitudinal Placebo—"Spillover" Group (all with own shoes)	8.72	84	.77608	.08468
	Running score with own shoes (Spillover Group)	8.59	84	.81179	.08857

Null hypothesis 3, states "there is no statistically significant difference on the mean running time of children measured seven days after Test 2, part II, and the running time at Baseline level" was confirmed. Based on the cumulative results of both groups, the null hypothesis cannot be rejected. However, for the Spillover group, the hypothesis test suggested that the running time measured seven days after the intervention was higher than the initial Baseline levels. In other words, seven days after the placebo intervention, participants in the spillover group ran slower than they had at the baseline level (their pre-conditioned normal running speed with their own shoes). This finding could be profound as it might suggest that the negative, spillover effect of the placebo in this experiment does carry on longer than the positive placebo effect.

Table 15.

Paired Samples Test—Spillover Group

				95% CI				
	M	*SD*	*SEM*	Lower	Upper	*t*	*df*	Sig. (2-tailed)
Test 2-Longitudinal Placebo (all with own shoes)—Running score with own shoes (Spillover Group)	.13262	.44443	.04849	.03617	.22907	2.74	83	.008

Note. CI= Confidence Interval

DISCUSSION

This study intended to investigate whether or not brand perception and affinity carries a placebo effect that not only impacts the performance of the brand user, but also that of individuals who are exposed to the brand but are unable to use it. Specifically, the study focused on following three research questions:

RQ1: Can brand recognition and perception lead to a placebo response that impacts product performance and efficacy among school children?

RQ2: Does the brand placebo effect demonstrated in RQ1, carry a spillover effect that impacts the performance of children who were exposed to the brand, but are unable to use it?

RQ3: Are brand-generated placebo and spillover effects a permanent phenomenon, or simply a temporary episode limited to the immediate time of exposure?

RQ1 (Can brand recognition and perception lead to a placebo response that impacts product performance and efficacy among school children?) was answered through the following hypothesis:

Hypothesis 1(a): Participants who are exposed to the superior attributes of the brand, and use it in the experiment, will experience a placebo effect, positively affecting their performance in a 50-meter run.

The findings of Test 1, Part II clearly indicated a significant improvement in the performance in the 50-meter run of participants who ran with the visible brand compared to their performance in Test1, Part I—brand elements invisible—(From M= 8.51 seconds to M=8.09 seconds). These findings affirm hypothesis 1(a), and provide a positive answer to RQ1, namely that brand recognition and perception lead to a placebo response that affects participants' performance with the brand. Considering that in Test 1, Part I (invisible brand elements) and Test 1, Part II (visible brand elements) the children were running with the exact same shoe, this indicates that merely the exposure to the brand elements and the children's affinity to the brand led to the significant difference in their performance.

RQ2 (Does the brand placebo effect demonstrated in RQ1, carry a spillover effect that impacts the performance of children who were exposed to the brand, but are unable to use it?) was answered by the following hypothesis:

Hypothesis 1(b): Participants who are exposed to the superior attributes of the brand, but do not use it in the experiment, will experience a spillover effect, negatively affecting their performance in a 50-meter run.

The findings of Test 1, Part II clearly indicated significant negative difference in the performance in the 50-meter run of participants who were exposed to the brand, but were unable to use it in the experiment (From *M*= 8.49 seconds in Test 1, Part I to *M*=8.76 seconds in Test 1, Part II). These findings affirm hypothesis 1(b), and provide a positive answer to RQ2, namely that participants who were exposed to the brand, but were unable to use it, experienced a spillover effect, negatively impacting their performance in the 50-meter run. This finding is in spite of the fact that in Test 1, Part I and Test 1, Part II all participants were running with the exact same shoe.

RQ1 and RQ2 were further supported by findings regarding the impact of participants' expressed expectation and motivation on the placebo and spillover effects displayed in Test 1, Part II. First, the impact of brand recognition and perception on participants' performance expectation and motivation was explored through the following hypothesis:

Hypothesis 2(a): Exposing participants to a brand's superior attributes will result in statistically significant differences in the motivation and performance expectation levels between participants who are able to use the brand and those who were exposed to the brand's superior attributes, but cannot use it.

Findings of the Mann Whitney analysis indicated significant differences between the two groups when the questions centered on their expectation and motivation regarding their performance with (or without) the brand (see Appendix A, Question 2; and Appendix B, Questions 1 and 2). In general, the Placebo group indicated high performance expectation and motivation levels, while the Spillover groups indicated low expectation and motivation levels.

However, no significant difference was found between the groups when asked to evaluate the brand, i.e., their expectation regarding the capability of the highlighted brand to impact their performance (see Appendix A, Question 1). Both groups indicated high expectation levels.

In order to substantiate the relationships between participants' levels of expectation and motivation and their ultimate performance the following hypothesis was tested:

Hypothesis 2(b): There is a statistically significant correlation between motivation and performance expectation scores and the performance difference in running time of participant in both Placebo and Spillover groups.

The Spearman Correlation test found a strong positive correlation between participants' expressed expectation and motivation and their performance in Test 1, Part II (50% of participants with "real" brand; 50% of participants with "knockoff" brand). These results further solidify the affirmative answers indicated for RQ1 and RQ2.

Finally, Research Question 3 (Are brand-generated placebo and spillover effects a permanent phenomenon, or simply a temporary episode limited to the immediate time of exposure?) was answered through the following hypothesis:

Hypothesis 3: There is a statistically significant difference on the mean running time of children measured seven days after initial intervention and the running time at baseline level.

The findings showed no significant difference (supporting the null hypothesis) in running times for the Placebo group, effectively indicating a waning placebo effect already seven days after its appearance. The findings, however, showed a significant difference in running time between Baseline and Test 2 (all running with own shoes) for the Spillover groups (Test 1, Part II participants who were exposed to the brand but unable to use it). Seven days after the intervention (and Spillover effect appearance), these participants had a significantly slower running time compared to Baseline. These findings support hypothesis 3 for the Spillover group, indicating that while the Placebo effect may be waning overtime, the spillover effect may have longitudinal attributes.

www.ingramcontent.com/pod-product-compliance
Lightning Source LLC
Chambersburg PA
CBHW062053270326
41931CB00013B/3060
9780999227404